Marriage
Personalities

DAVID FIELD

HARVEST HOUSE PUBLISHERS
Eugene, Oregon 97402

Names of persons and details of situations have been changed to protect the privacy of the individuals involved.

Except where otherwise indicated, all Scripture quotations in this book are taken from the New American Standard Bible, © The Lockman Foundation 1960, 1962, 1963, 1968, 1971, 1972, 1973, 1975, 1977. Used by permission.

MARRIAGE PERSONALITIES

Copyright © 1986 by David Field
Published by Harvest House Publishers
Eugene, Oregon 97402

Library of Congress Catalog Card Number 85-60127
Trade edition ISBN 0-89081-476-7
Cloth edition ISBN 0-89081-546-1

Printed in the United States of America.

ACKNOWLEDGMENTS

Writing a book is a team effort. My parents, Gene and Jo Ann Field, are wonderful—hardworking and supportive of their children. Thanks, Mom and Dad! Debby, my sister, displays great loyalty. What I took for granted—a secure, loving family —still works in me today as I "rub shoulders" with my wife, Lonna, and the three fine children that God has given in my life: Tory, Jonathan, and Dana. Lonna's parents, Lon and Ruth Setser, have always been people who have believed in us enthusiastically. My family and all my patients have given me cause to write this book on marriage.

I want to thank the publishers for their confidence in my materials. This project was in the hands of a few very special people who worked behind the scenes. Carol Manley and Carl Heuss typed and retyped. Diane Wilson read chapters and edited. Betty Allbee, my secretary, served as head of the "encouragement bureau." Thank you, team!

To Lonna—
My God-provided special partner

CONTENTS

CHAPTER 1

Marriage Opportunities

It had been a full but satisfying day. As my last two patients left the office, I loosened my tie, unbuttoned my collar, and leaned back at my desk to catch my breath before heading home. Eight solid hours of counseling was draining work, yet I wasn't quite ready to call it a day. I wanted to review the cases I had handled.

I thought about my first appointment with a young woman who had been married only two years. Joan complained about the loss of love and affection for her husband. She was infatuated with a fellow employee and wanted to know if God could lead her out of her present marriage and into another one. As I probed, I learned how she was deeply hurt by her husband's inability to attend to her emotional needs. As a result she had built a wall around herself, and gradually the warm, loving feelings for him had deteriorated. She hadn't gone looking for an affair, but the fellow employee had tried to help her, and in the process they had fallen in love.

It didn't take long for me to realize that Joan was in an Active-Passive marriage relationship, with elements of a Kid's marriage also present. She was frustrated that her husband would not take an active role in the relationship, and her immaturity had led her to look elsewhere for fulfillment. As I reviewed with her the dynamics of a third-party relationship, I explained that—based on my years of experience as a counselor—the likelihood of it succeeding was remote. Also, she would miss out on a significant opportunity for personal development if she escaped from her marriage relationship. When our hour was up, she agreed to bring her husband with her to the next appointment.

9

My second hour was spent with both Jim and Lori. For the first 15 minutes Jim harangued about how their kids were out of control and his wife was responsible for the lack of discipline. The longer he talked, the more visibly deflated Lori became, until she seemed almost like molded Jello in the chair next to him. When Jim finished his tirade, I asked Lori to respond, and she sadly said that it was impossible to talk to her husband. "When I don't agree with him, he just says I don't know what I'm talking about. So we don't talk."

This was a classic Macho marriage. Jim had so dominated his wife that she no longer believed she was a significant person. Lori needed to be encouraged by our session, to realize that she could assert herself for her own well-being and the good of their marriage. And Jim had to realize he was destroying the marriage. He needed to support his wife's attempts to parent. "Of course, you don't have to follow my advice," I told him. "But if you do, it will make a big difference."

Right before lunch, Steve and Joyce had come for their fourth appointment. They were in their midthirties, both talented individuals, active in the community. There was no doubt about their love and commitment to each other. Their problem was stress. They were involved in too many good activities to the detriment of their children and marriage. "We've done the assignment," Steve reported. "Here's what we've cut out of our schedule. And this is our plan for spending more quality time with our children." I couldn't help but be pleased. Here was an Active-Active marriage—two people taking full responsibility for their lives, and learning some new skills to make themselves a better couple.

My first appointment after lunch was with a woman who had left her husband, though I sensed that she really still loved him. Carla had been very dependent upon her family, especially her father, as a child. When she married, she transferred that dependence to her spouse. After three years of marriage, she woke up one day to realize that she felt more like a child than an adult. And that made her furious. She realized that no one had ever let her make a decision. She was determined to begin deciding what she was going to do with her own life.

Carla was the victim of a Helper-Helpee relationship. Actually, she had the right idea for solving her dependency problem, but was going about it in the wrong manner. We reviewed some ways that she could assert herself without cutting herself off from those she loved.

Then there was Tony and Gwenn. This sharp-looking couple entered my office and sat on opposite sides of the room, like two gladiators ready for battle. They admitted they argued most of the time, yet neither had filed for a divorce. Obviously, neither was about to surrender an inch to the other. I couldn't resist a chuckle as I recalled how I turned to Tony about ten minutes into our session and asked, "Is it possible that you're so stubborn that you won't admit any mistakes because you don't want to give your wife the upper hand?" He quickly answered, "I'm sure it is." Then I turned to Gwenn and said, "And I bet you're just as stubborn as your husband." She agreed.

Here was yet another marriage personality—the Active-Resistant couple. Tony and Gwenn were a difficult case because their greatest strength—their strong individual personalities—was also their greatest weakness. It would be a challenge to help them learn to become vulnerable to each another.

The final session of the day was with a middle-aged couple who had drifted off the beaten path in their marriage. This was their final session after six months of counseling, and in many respects it was a victory celebration. When Darrall and Bonnie first came to me, she felt neglected by her husband, and he felt smothered by her constant badgering. Now that tension was gone. They related some of their successes in the past few weeks, how they had worked through disagreements, and the fact that today she was able to be open with her husband, and he felt close to her without being crowded.

When Darrall and Bonnie had first come to my office, I had sensed that theirs was another Active-Passive relationship. They still have an Active-Passive marriage, but it is working much better. Before they left, we prayed together and thanked God that He had enabled this marriage to function well again, and asked Him to use them to encourage other couples.

This was not an unusual day. Each of these people had a unique marriage personality. A few years ago I might have tried to counsel these couples in similar ways. But none of them could be placed into a singular package called marriage, given some universal pat answers, and sent home with all their problems solved. Success with these patients came by recognizing them as people with different marriage personalities, and adjusting the treatment to fit those personalities.

Perhaps you've never considered the fact that your marriage has a personality. Sure, your marriage is different from every other marriage. But there are certain characteristics—how you relate to each other, your family backgrounds, the way you handle pressure—that give it a certain personality. Realizing the dynamics of that personality can help you understand your relationship and how to better relate to your spouse.

Many couples I meet with have what I call an "average" marriage. They aren't great, but they aren't ready to call it quits either. Unfortunately in our society, we find it hard to accept being "average." I want to assure you that average is okay. It means that there are good times and bad times. There are strengths and there are weaknesses. There are marriages in worse shape than yours, and marriages in better shape. In any case, your marriage has room to grow.

My goal in writing this book is to help you face your marriage the way it really is. Perhaps you've read other marriage books or attended seminars that "preached" an ideal for marriage. You may think that every marriage should be a heavenly experience, and that if yours isn't, there's something drastically wrong. The truth is that every marriage has struggles, and few are photogenic. So let's deal with the reality of your marriage instead of trying to make it fit the perfect model.

At times you may find this book a little like surgery. When we go to the hospital for an operation, the purpose is to improve our physical health. I've had four operations in my life, and each time when I woke up in the recovery room, I felt worse than before the surgery. But in each case, as I allowed time for healing, I experienced significant improvement, and the end result was that I functioned better.

You may find that minor or major surgery is necessary in your marriage. It is admittedly painful when the scalpel digs into your relationship. What you read in this book may not always be pleasant. But my prayer is that God will use what I say to cut away some of the nagging discomfort and help you enjoy a healthier marriage.

Even if your spouse doesn't cooperate, you will not find it a futile effort. I believe it is the responsibility of every person to do as good a job as possible in the marriage relationship, whether the spouse cooperates or not. When we become Christians, surrendering our lives to the control and authority of Jesus Christ, we assume the responsibility for developing and maintaining our own spiritual lives.

That responsibility continues even though we're married. Some people forget that they are still to take care of themselves as a person, spiritually and in other ways. When they shift that responsibility to their spouse, and expect their fulfillment in life from that relationship, they are disappointed. I can never legitimately place the responsibility for my Christian life on anyone else's shoulders. It is mine and mine alone. I will be the first to recognize and accept the fact that my environment, including my spouse, will influence my attitudes and my motivation about growing in my relationship with Christ. But it's not the partner's responsibility; my spiritual dignity is maintained and developed only as I take responsibility for my spiritual walk with God.

Most of us would like to believe that marriage should be a haven of rest, a place of retreat, and a source of energy. Somehow it seems unfair that marriage can produce rumblings, difficulties, disagreements, and disappointments. Perhaps the biggest challenge you'll face in this book is the idea that your marriage difficulties are significant opportunities. No, I don't have a persecution complex. I'm simply stating a fact based on years of counseling couples who have marital problems. I've concluded that problems in marriage—things that seem beyond our ability to cope—make us eligible to experience God's power through His Holy Spirit. If you're willing, marital struggles can strengthen you as you work through them, thereby producing growth.

I'm not suggesting that just because you allow Christ to work in you, there will be immediate improvement in your marriage. God promises to bless us if we follow Him and obey Him, but we do that not for the changes, but because He is worthy. God will use the problems in our marriages to develop our individual walk with Him. That's why I can say with confidence when people come into my office: "I realize that this is extremely painful. You would rather have almost anything happen to you besides marriage problems. But I want to remind you that in the midst of your problems, the two of you are on the verge of the greatest opportunity you've had yet in your marriage, for this will force you to become more dependent upon Jesus Christ and His power to work in and through you.''

So don't run away from your marital problems. I'm hoping that this book will help you see that you are not alone in your struggles, and that God provides the resources to help you enjoy a happy, healthy marriage. It begins by realizing that all marriages are *not* alike. We're going to examine seven common marriage personalities, and in the process, you will no doubt find that you fit one of those seven styles. You'll see where you have strengths and weaknesses, and receive some suggestions for making your marriage stronger.

We will also look at some common marital detours that are reflected to some degree in most or all of the personalities. And then we'll talk about some basic skills that can help you better relate to your mate.

In the back of the book I've enclosed a Marital Assessment Questionnaire. I encourage you and your mate to take this test in order to help you see the strengths and weaknesses of your marriage. I've used this questionnaire with a wide cross-section of people, so when you've tabulated your score, you'll see how your marriage compares with other marriages. It's not a hard and fast assessment, and it's certainly not perfect. Its primary purpose is to give you a feel for where you fit on a continuum between a healthy-optimal relationship and one that may be struggling.

By now you're probably curious to launch into the marriage personalities. But first we need to have a framework for our discussion. So we're going to take a look at what constitutes a healthy marriage. Then, as we look at each personality, we'll be able to see where it tends to be stronger or weaker in terms of our model. So let's get started!

CHAPTER 2

Characteristics of a Healthy Marriage

When a mother retains a piano teacher for her child, she expects the instructor to teach the child the keyboard, use of the pedals, how to read music, and a general understanding of music theory. The teacher would be remiss if he or she told all the things not to do on the piano but never taught the student the right way to use the instrument. Obviously, the only way to effectively teach piano is for the teacher to show the student how to do the things that he or she expects. Once the student knows the standard, it's much easier to recognize when he's doing it wrong.

The same is true in marriage. It's easy to examine the problems in marriage without knowing the guidelines for a healthy relationship. What do I mean by a healthy marriage? I define a healthy marriage as:

> TWO PEOPLE WHO HAVE COMMITTED THEM-
> SELVES TO TAKE INDIVIDUAL RESPONSIBILITY
> TO WORK TOGETHER FOR THE FULFILLMENT
> OF EACH OTHER.

In other words, a healthy relationship requires two people, each vitally interested in and committed to the betterment of the other.

Many couples have firsthand experience with what doesn't work. But what are the criteria by which they evaluate what they are doing? Several studies, plus the experience of marriage counselors around the country, have led to a general consensus as to what contributes to a healthy marriage. These seven characteristics will serve as reference points as you

15

evaluate your marriage and the various marriage personalities.

It is my belief that the healthier the marriage, the more the relationship will demonstrate these seven qualities. There is no particular reason for the order in which these characteristics are listed; they are simply integral parts of a fully functioning, rich relationship. When one or more of these elements are missing, the marriage suffers.

Characteristic Number 1: Time Together

It is imperative that a couple have unhindered time together. This needs to be both structured and casual. Structured time falls into the category of planned vacations, weekends, or "dates." This time has the advantage of allowing the couple to have the relationship regularly nurtured.

Casual exchange can occur in the kitchen after dinner, perhaps when both are helping clean the dishes, or when a person returns home from work or a shopping excursion. It's a time for expressing appreciation to each other and keeping each other informed about the details of your lives.

A relationship cannot maintain its health unless the husband and wife continue to have meaningful contact. This contact exercises the marital muscles. When a cast has been placed on a broken limb, the muscles tend to atrophy because they are not used. In the same way, the relationship muscles shrivel up without the exercise of time together.

Because of the pace of our society, time together does not just happen automatically. When couples spend time together, it is usually because they fought through the jungle of time commitments to set aside that special weekend or "date." In addition, when they do find a few casual moments together, they take advantage of that precious time.

It is one thing to arrange time together; it is quite another to *want* to be together. Couples can go through the motions of establishing time together, but this doesn't always mean that they enjoy it. Couples with a healthy relationship honestly enjoy being together. They are like giant electromagnets, drawing each other into their own magnetic field.

No one, not even the best marriage therapist, understands what causes that magnetism. But we do know that it happens.

The couples who enjoy being together and schedule time to do so are happier and healthier in their relationship.

Characteristic Number 2: Spiritual Emphasis

Couples who recognize that there is a God and that He is actively involved in their lives tend to have healthier marriages. They not only recognize God as a viable agent in their lives, but also attempt to live in a way that is pleasing to Him. Often this means having to adapt themselves to change and personal development. In attempting to please God, moral behavior is influenced daily by His direction, with an emphasis on being kind, selfless, and cooperative with family as well as with all people in our society. This spiritual emphasis provides a common reference point for moral and ethical behavior that goes beyond each individual. In other words, both of them look to their spiritual principles as guidelines for behavior. Hopefully this influences their motivation to adapt to the other person without always having their own way.

When two people do not have a similar spiritual value system and are not involved together in some sort of spiritual activity, they are more vulnerable to difficulties. Very simply, a spiritual emphasis plays a significant part in a person's values with regard to marriage. Self-sacrifice and forgiveness are integral parts of most spiritual value systems, and are applicable to married life. That's not to say that a couple which does not have a spiritual emphasis cannot have a fairly successful marriage. Many do. However, those who subscribe to a spiritual emphasis tend to function better because it serves as a significant common ground.

As two individuals are submissive to Christ and desire to please Him, there is a positive spillover onto the marriage. This does not mean that one person must believe exactly like the other in regard to all spiritual matters. But if they try to be Christlike, they will think the best of the other, not need to defend themselves, and consider each other as equally important in God's sight. Acting that way endows them with more potential for marital harmony than those who are not striving to be Christlike.

Of course, we all occasionally offend our spouses. Sometimes they are hurt by what we do even though it was unintentional.

The Bible says clearly that we are to forgive other people as we have been forgiven by Christ. The Bible also clearly instructs an individual to seek forgiveness from the person he has offended. If a person is serious about being Christlike, then he must be serious about seeking forgiveness from his spouse whom he has offended. This very act of Christlikeness maintains harmony in any marriage relationship. Forgiveness is like the shortening that keeps bread or cake from sticking to a pan and burning in the oven.

Scripture provides guidelines for the basic foundational structure of a marriage relationship. These foundational principles include marriage permanence, partnership, roles, and responsibilities, and serve as a model to all couples. This structure protects the couple and helps them stay on track.

However, within these guidelines every marriage will exhibit unique expression. When I say the word "chair," you may picture a solid-oak, straight backed kitchen chair. Or you may picture the most comfortable family room easy chair. Another person might visualize a slow-moving rocking chair. No one can debate that all three mental pictures are valid, yet they are quite different.

The same is true of spiritual guidelines for marriage: The principles apply to all, but they are implemented differently in each marriage. Two men who desire to show love to their wives—a biblical principle—may do so in different ways. One may express it with flowers and a special night out, while another may take care of the kids so she can have a night free to go shopping. Both are valid expressions of love.

Characteristic Number 3: Negotiating Ability

The ability to listen and respond without defensiveness is imperative to the success of any marriage. Responsive listening is not just hearing words, but observing body language. Communication can happen with a hug, a held hand, a pat on the back, or a walk in the park together. Though marital communication is not exclusively dependent upon words, there are times when it is necessary for individuals to confront the issues at hand.

Good communication requires two individuals—one who is expressing his thoughts and feelings while the other listens without responding prematurely. The listener's job is to attempt to understand what his spouse is saying. To turn away, reduce eye contact, pout, or in any way ignore the speaker is nonproductive. Effective listening respects a partner's point of view, whether you agree with it or not.

Just because one person thinks something is true does not necessarily mean that it is. In any marriage relationship, two people can have an identical experience and yet describe it differently. One view of what happened is not necessarily complete. Therefore, we need to understand how our partner sees things. Whether we agree with what one sees is not as important as trying to understand his vantage point, while demonstrating respect by listening to him. Healthy negotiation takes two people who are committed to the process. This is a learned skill for most people, and we will devote a full chapter to it later.

Characteristic Number 4: Maturity

A marriage that functions successfully usually involves individuals who are somewhat mature. This maturity allows them to be submissive and responsive to each other. Because they feel good about themselves, they do not need to be defensive but can honestly learn and respond to the frustrations, joys, and victories of their partner. Unfortunately, maturity doesn't automatically happen at any prearranged, postadolescent life phase.

A mature individual is humble rather than self-willed, resistant, negative, and uncooperative. He is willing to admit error and learn from other people. While he loves himself, he also admits his weakness and humbles himself before God and others. Maturity also speaks of loyalty, that special respect for another individual which leads to confidentiality. Loyalty means that one partner does not emotionally "undress" his mate in front of other people. To constantly gossip and complain about our spouses erodes the marriage commitment.

Maturity also involves persevering in the midst of disappointment and hurt. No marriage goes the way we want it to all the time. Just as a farmer adjusts when bad weather hurts his crop, so couples must learn how to persevere through the difficult, frustrating, and disappointing times of marriage.

Finally, maturity is the willingness to seek help from others. Occasionally problems in a relationship seem overwhelming. The willingness to seek help is not a sign of weakness but a sign of wisdom. It is impossible for me to know everything about computers without instruction. Similarly, wise couples realize they don't know everything about marriage. We can love our spouse and want the best in our relationship without fully understanding how to produce that result. The wise couple studies strong marriages, attends seminars, seeks counsel, or reads books in order to strengthen their relationship.

Characteristic Number 5: Play and Humor

It may seem ironic to suggest play and humor as part of a healthy marriage relationship, especially after talking about maturity. However, people who are mature have the capacity for fun. We all know that life occasionally throws curves at us. Sometimes the best way to deal with hurts and disappointments is to laugh. Laughter is healthy because it relieves tension and helps us accept reality.

Also, it is simply fun to have a good time! A couple that exercises together or plays a sport or game or goes out to mutually enjoyable activities can often prevent relationship paralysis.

Humor is similar to play and involves warmhearted and nonsarcastic teasing. Practical jokes and laughing at ourselves and others is humor in action.

A lady who lived near the outskirts of a city recognized the value of humor. One day she found a donkey in her front yard. She called the humane society and asked them to come and pick it up. When the two men arrived, she changed her mind and asked instead if they would rope the donkey and take it to her upstairs bathroom. At first they refused, but she was persistent and persuasive. After the donkey was placed in the bathroom, they couldn't resist asking her why she was doing this. She answered, "My husband always comes home, plops down in his overstuffed chair, takes off his shoes, grabs the paper, and asks, 'What's new?' Tonight I'm going to tell him!"

Characteristic Number 6: Intimacy

My mother used to make the best chocolate cake in the neighborhood—at least in my opinion. Chocolate cake just wasn't chocolate cake without Mom's special peanut butter chocolate frosting on it. To me, intimacy in marriage is like the peanut butter frosting on that chocolate cake. It's knowing and being vulnerable to another individual. The very nature of intimacy implies that it is private. Throughout our lives we are intimate with only a very few people. There may be one, two, or ten people with whom we develop a close relationship. Unfortunately, some people never develop a close relationship with anyone.

Intimacy involves appreciation, attraction, physical encounter, and prayer. It means being known on the inside as well as the outside. It is allowing yourself to be appreciated by your lover and to thoroughly and honestly enjoy her appreciation of you. Intimacy requires sharing inner thoughts and feelings with each other. It happens when two people are able to pray together about their own frailties, insufficiencies, hopes, and dreams.

Intimacy also involves sexually pleasing each other. Just because two people have a sexual encounter does not mean that they have been intimate. Intimacy in the bedroom happens when each partner not only receives physical pleasure but also gives physical pleasure. The focus is not on getting sex but on giving sex. It is true that many spouses, instead of enjoying sex, fake it because they are unable or unwilling to talk about what feels good to them. That very resistance prevents sexual intimacy.

It is vital not only to be sexually educated but to also become a student of what pleases your spouse. And there is no way to do this without adequate time for foreplay—not only in the bedroom but also prior to going into the bedroom. In our fast-paced society, it has become increasingly difficult to shift gears from parenting pressure and vocational concerns to have an electric sexual encounter.

Every marriage has its own built-in cues to signal each other when they want to get together. Some raise their eyebrows or have a certain kind of smile. Others even have a schedule. There is really no right or wrong way to let each other know that you want to have sex as long as it is clearly understood and adaptable to your situation.

Finally, sexual intimacy does not mean perfect sex. It means two people who willfully and playfully work to please each other. The goal is not perfect sex but mutual pleasure.

Characteristic Number 7: Commitment

Commitment serves as the cornerstone of marriage. Without an intentional, persevering, and complete commitment to the relationship, it can become vulnerable to emotional and/or legal divorce. There is nothing so solid as two people who have individually and intentionally committed themselves to a marriage relationship "for better or worse, for richer or poorer, in sickness and in health, till death do them part." This commitment goes beyond circumstances because it is completely unconditional.

Genuine commitment is an individual choice. Any commitment oriented around self-satisfaction tends to be unstable simply because people tend to stay in the relationship only as long as it feels good or meets their personal needs. Healthy and permanent love is characterized by my choosing to love someone. That choice is dependent upon my integrity rather than my partner's performance. Does this mean I always have warm, mushy feelings? Hardly! It means that as my feelings fluctuate, my commitment overrides my feelings.

Commitment involves exclusiveness. It says that no one else will be a part of our intimate relationship. It places the other partner in a "numero uno" position. Not only is the partner important, but also the relationship itself. The two individuals and their relationship are equally honored.

Trust is that part of the commitment in which two people entrust their lives to the relationship without any reserve or hesitation. Trust is built not so much on the trustworthiness of a spouse as on trust in ourselves to live consistently with our own values and commitment. It is not possible to make another person trustworthy, so we must work on being trustworthy ourselves.

In cases where trust is an issue, the problem usually resides within the person struggling to trust, not the object of trust. This does not apply to all cases, nor does it excuse the behavior of the one who is the object of trust. If she does not feel she can trust him because he has failed her in the past, then he needs to "clean up his act" and become a faithful partner. But her struggle with trust will not be resolved automatically because he acts responsibly.

Commitment also has to do with the power balance of a relationship. It is easy for the balance in a relationship to be upended when either party is overly self-consumed. A marriage made up of individuals who are self-oriented usually gravitates to one of two extremes—married singles with either too much overt individuality or else fusion, with loss of individuality.

Married Single   Merging Marriage

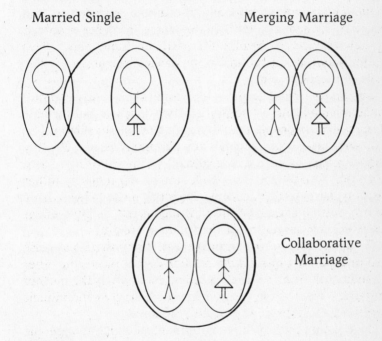

Collaborative
Marriage

The diagram shows the extremes of over-self-commitment. Married singles are mutually self-oriented. They demonstrate their lack of commitment to the relationship by being first concerned and committed to themselves, then secondarily committed to their spouse and the relationship. Consequently, they are not inside the marriage circle but on the very edge. Often one partner is a married single while the other is inside the marriage circle.

The other extreme, that of being self-involved, is called fusion or merging. Although the two parties of a merging couple are inside the marriage circle, they are overinvolved with each another. They are depending too much on the other person to fulfill their needs, which is also an expression of selfishness.

The healthy relationship is the collaborative marriage relationship. Here two people have individually committed themselves to the marriage relationship and have stepped inside the marriage circle. They remain within the marriage boundaries because they continue to choose to do so. They maintain their own individuality, yet work together as a team. They are not overly dependent upon each other, nor are they trying to escape from each other. The optimal marital commitment is demonstrated by the collaborative relationship in which both people are cooperatively committed to each other and to Jesus Christ.

In summary, healthy marriages are not made up of people who live under the illusion of having a perfect marriage, nor do they need to be married to the perfect partner. Instead, healthy marriages consist of people who are committed to the process of growing and living together. They are dedicated to understanding and adjusting to each other. They accept the complex task of mutual adjustment.

Within that context, there are a variety of marriage personalities. Now that we've established the criteria for healthy marriages, let's examine these personalities. In the process, we will see how these characteristics are upheld or weakened. My prayer is that this information will help you enjoy a healthier marriage.

CHAPTER 3

Marriage Personalities

I am awed by the fact that every marriage is a unique relationship. There has never been and never will be a relationship exactly the same as that between you and your spouse.

If every marriage is unique, then where does the concept of marriage personalities come in? We can note that every individual is unique, yet mental health professionals have identified several personality and behavioral categories. In the same way, marriage and family therapists have observed that marriages can be grouped into categories. Those categories are determined by the similar behavior styles that exist in marriage relationships.

Instead of seeing marriage as a large, undefined mass of relationships, it helps us position couples into categories for better understanding. There is enough observable evidence to classify marriages, and I do not believe that it offends the uniqueness of a marriage to say that couples are similar to other married couples. In fact, sometimes it helps couples to know that they are not alone, that they are not the only ones who struggle with a certain set of problems.

Recently more and more people I know have had a color analysis. There are skin tones, hair colors, eye colors, and other factors that affect how the colors of clothing look on different individuals. After a person has her colors analyzed, she receives a color chart which helps her pick out clothes that compliment her.

But dividing people into four different color groupings doesn't mean they lose their unique identity. My wife is a "Winter." She has her chart and buys her clothes according to that chart. As I understand it, my wife is not like every other

"Winter." Her basic (primary) colors are the same, but her accent (secondary) colors are different, which allows her to develop a unique wardrobe.

Marriage personalities work in much the same way. The following are seven marriage personality types I have uncovered from research and my clinical experience.

> **ACTIVE-PASSIVE**: This is the most common personality (approximately 28 percent of all marriages). It consists of an aggressive partner (usually the wife), who diligently strives to make the marriage work, and a passive partner, who is led or directed.
>
> **ACTIVE-RESISTANT** (24 percent): Consists of two talented, strong-willed individuals, one who is aggressively seeking closeness in the relationship and the one who is actively resisting the effort.
>
> **HELPER-HELPEE** (8 percent): This relationship is sustained by the fact that one person (the helpee) needs the other (the helper).
>
> **MACHO** (12 percent): One partner (almost always the husband) totally dominates this marriage.
>
> **KIDS** (5 percent): This is a marriage between two immature "kids" who are not ready to cope with the pressures of life. They need outside help, often from their parents, in order to survive.
>
> **PRETENSE** (3 percent): This is the rarest category. It is a "make-believe" marriage between two people who have no romantic attraction to each other. They have totally different backgrounds, interests, goals, and values.
>
> **ACTIVE-ACTIVE** (20 percent): This marriage is founded on a firm commitment to each other, and both partners are equipped and motivated to make the marriage work.

The above percentages are not based on clinical research but on my own observation as a counselor. (Other counselors have encountered similar results.) Each marriage personality category has its own set of characteristics that differentiates it from others. In the chapters devoted to each specific marriage personality, I point out those unique characteristics as well as the outward style, inward experience, strengths, weaknesses, and ways to improve the marriage.

You probably have a few questions about marriage personalities. First of all, what are the ingredients that go into shaping a marriage personality? One major ingredient is the personality of the two individuals involved in the marriage. If one partner is highly assertive, capable, and directed while the other is somewhat passive, indecisive, and searching, that will affect the chemistry of their marriage.

Another factor is the condition of the two people when they meet. This includes their maturity, ages, and current life circumstances—whether good or not so good. A person's history—life events, both positive and traumatic—also affects how he or she approaches a marriage relationship. The family experience (I frequently refer to it as "the family of origin") also affects each individual. A person's perception of his parents' marriage will influence what he expects from his own marriage relationship. If the parents constantly argued and fought, a person may do the same, or possibly overreact and refuse to confront any conflicts.

Also of utmost importance are our values and beliefs. For example, if the husband believes in settling disagreements immediately and his wife doesn't, that is a conflict of values which affects the resolution style of the marriage.

Education and intelligence also play a part in the development of a marriage personality. They influence values, negotiating style, and whether or not the relationship is competitive (struggle for control), unilateral (one person in control), or bilateral (shared control).

A couple's social and religious environment affects their marriage personality. If a newly married couple from a strong ethnic background continues to live in that ethnic community, they are expected to be like other marriages in that community. Social status—whether yuppie, religious fanatic, blue collar, or socially elite—also influences a marriage.

Does a marriage personality ever change? Not usually. Just as the personality of a child is developed between six months and six years of age, the basic marriage personality is formed during the mutual accommodation stage (premarital through two years postmarital). After that there are refinements, but most changes have to do with adjusting to life demands rather than with changing the basic marriage-behavior style.

Exceptions are the Kids' marriage and occasionally the Pretense marriage. A couple in a Kids' marriage, if they survive, usually grow up and shift gears to another marriage personality. On less frequent occasions, couples in Pretense marriages shift gears to another personality slot. The basic personality of the other five kinds of marriage will usually not change dramatically, but the degree of marital health may fluctuate.

Does every marriage fit into one of the seven marriage personality categories? Definitely not. Some marriages defy all definition and understanding. The concept of marriage personalities is only one way (and I believe a very good way) to promote a better understanding of marriage itself. It would be presumptuous for anyone to say that we fully understand marriages and that every marriage fits into one of these marriage personalities. Yet most marriages clearly reflect one specific marriage personality or a combination of two of them.

Are there degrees of marital strengths and weaknesses within marriage personalities? Yes. We might compare it to a blue house. There are many shades of blue. One home might be painted pastel blue and another a rich lake blue.

As you read the description of your marriage personality, you will get a feeling for whether your marriage typifies all the strengths and/or weaknesses of that personality. You will also get feedback on the health of your marriage from the previous chapter and the common marital detours in Chapter 11.

You may ask, "Can my marriage fit into more than one category?" Certainly. If someone asked you the color of your home, instead of saying "light blue" or "dark blue," you might answer "blue-green." Just as a home can be a mixture of two basic colors, so a couple's marriage can be a combination, such as Active-Passive and Helper-Helpee. Generally, however, I do not find that couples mirror more than two of the distinct marriage personalities.

Note that I have not said anything about men and women fitting into particular roles in marriage. The issue we are addressing is how each partner behaves in relationship to the other, regardless of the sex. Certainly there are identifiable differences between the sexes due to biological and cultural influence. However, in marriage personalities the emphasis is upon the role itself, not the sex of the person who fills that role. One Active-Passive marriage could have the husband in the active role while another marriage could have the wife as the active spouse. The only exception is the Macho marriage, where the man almost always fills the macho role.

As you read each of the chapters on the seven marriage personalities, it is important that you keep an open mind. It does not work to read about each personality and then decide which one you *want* to be. You need to decide which one you *are*. It is important to accept ownership of your marriage personality, with both its pleasant and unpleasant aspects, for that is the starting point for improving the relationship.

In order to adequately paint a picture of each marriage personality, I tell a story about a couple who typifies that marriage personality. I describe their beginning, outward style (the way they look to other people), inward experience (thoughts and feelings), some of their strengths and weaknesses, and some suggestions for improving the marriage.

In limited space we cannot describe each personality to the degree that it fits every marriage. However, in reading each "model," there should be enough information to give you a strong indication as to which personality best describes your marriage. To help you make an accurate decision, I have pointed out almost all the negative aspects of each personality. Not every marriage has all of these, nor are they all severe. But left unchecked, they can and probably will get worse.

Finally, I've tried to give a few suggestions for each personality. But you'll also note that some problem areas, common to several personalities, require more detailed discussion. I hope you'll take advantage of the latter chapters to work on one or more of these areas.

Now let's proceed with our examination of the marriage personalities, beginning with the most common.

CHAPTER 4

The Active-Passive Marriage

If you watch reruns of the old "Honeymooners" TV show or read the "Dagwood" comic strip, you're aware of the Active-Passive marriage. Art Carney and Dagwood play the classic role of passive husbands. Such men have borne the brunt of jokes for centuries, like the one about Joe, who attended a marriage seminar. There were two registration lines, one for henpecked husbands and the other for nonhenpecked husbands. When Joe bypassed the longer henpecked line, one of his friends yelled, "Hey, Joe, what are you doing in that line?" Joe answered, "My wife told me this is where I belong."

Active-Passive marriages are the most common of the seven marriage personality types. Most people, when asked to describe a typical American marriage, identify one or more characteristics of this relationship. The active partner pushes or prods the passive partner to make the marriage and family work; the passive partner feels corralled, directed, or even henpecked. Sometimes the husband is the active partner, but usually the man is the passive one who constantly feels nagged. Let's examine a typical case.

Tom and Susan have been married for 20 years. Both are frustrated with the marriage, yet they trudge forward, sometimes despairing, sometimes comfortable. Tom is tired of being unfavorably compared to Susan's father and brother. It seems that every attempt to please her is either too little, too much, too late, or too soon. While Tom still loves Susan, he is disheartened by her nagging and complaining and has stopped reaching out to her. Instead, he retreats from the "combat zone" and loses himself in a hobby or television.

They met in high school when Tom was a senior and Susan

31

a sophomore. He had a slight, five-foot-nine-inch frame, a pleasing smile, and short, brown, oiled hair. He said little in or out of class and never caused problems for any of his teachers. Susan was friendly, responsible, conforming, and energetic. She was neither a party girl nor a prude. Teachers liked her because she participated in class and was genuinely interested in learning.

When they began to date, it was Susan's openness and attentiveness that helped the relationship take root. At times he waited for her after school while she finished a project for the yearbook or the debate team. Tom was not pushy and always treated Susan with respect. After awhile their dates became ritualistic—movie, drag Main Street, and a snack at the local hamburger stand.

After graduation, Tom spent a year at a technical school, then returned home to a job at a local business. In the meantime Susan discovered "life" beyond their commuity and decided she wanted more than the mundane routine of a small town.

Their engagement was unusual. Tom couldn't find the words to ask her to marry him, so he didn't. Instead, he said things like "How many children would you like to have?" and "If we get married, spring would be a nice time for the wedding." One Saturday afternoon Tom and Susan examined a display of rings at a jewelry store. When Susan mentioned that one was particularly appealing, Tom returned later and purchased it. He let her discover the ring in the glove compartment of his car by saying, "Honey, would you get a Kleenex for me, please?" She found the ring, smiled, and gave him a big hug.

Unfortunately, the manner in which they decided to marry became a pattern for dealing with all important interpersonal issues. Tom found it difficult to express his feelings because he was easily embarrassed. It was easier for him when Susan made the first move and he responded. They had a small wedding because he was uncomfortable among crowds. Though Susan wanted a large wedding, she thought to herself, "I'll respect his wishes. After all, a small wedding will be easier on my parents too."

After one year of marriage, it was obvious to Susan that Tom's job was not going anywhere and that her own opportunities were limited. Tom liked his work, but it was not paying the bills. When he failed to look for better employment, Susan took matters into her own hands, found him a job in the city, and insisted that they move. Tom hated his new job but would not do anything about it except secretly blame his wife. As he retreated from her, Susan took on more domestic duties— home chores, finances, responsibility for "baby-prevention," and maintaining relationships with in-laws and friends. She constantly found herself taking the initiative in their marriage. When they needed more money, she went to work. When they needed a larger home for children, she found it and arranged for a loan at the bank. When the kids needed a church, she found one with a good Sunday school program.

They were not that unhappy for the first 12 years of their marriage. However, Susan began to run out of energy as she rehearsed her disappointments: "I get so tired of trying to keep this family together by myself. I wish he'd show more interest." Tom's mental tape deck projected scenes of her disapproval and nagging, and of always surrendering to what she wanted. As a result, resentment mounted and distance increased.

After years of little direct communication, Tom and Susan lack confidence in their ability to deal with each other. Not that Susan hasn't tried a few things. She has read several books and articles and even attended a marriage workshop. Occasionally she "lets him have it." Other times she shares her problems with friends or family while seeking advice or consolation. When they do talk, Tom and Susan concentrate on subjects like the kids, dinner menus, news items, church programs, or work.

Sex is sporadic and tense. Tom "wants it" but is not confident enough to pursue it unless she gives him some cue. Sex is also frustrating for Susan. Her conscience says that it is her duty but her feelings are confused. She does not want him to touch her while at the same time she desperately wants to be touched and loved. When they do have sex they perform with little or no foreplay and Susan climaxes infrequently, which further intimidates Tom's sense of masculinity.

Susan's emotions are mixed—disillusionment, disappointment, anger, guilt, loneliness—yet she remains hopeful and determined. In fact, underneath it all, Tom and Susan still care for each other. But they seem unable to break through the crust of hurt and disappointment.

• • •

Active-Passive marriages vary in marital fulfillment. However, I rarely find them exceptionally good or bad. They make up the middle road—typical relationships with their share of ups and downs. These marriages consist of good, conscientious, down-to-earth people. Most of the time their relationship has a casual flow. When there is a major disappointment for the active partner, he or she is likely to get on the passive partner's case in a big way. Otherwise this relationship is characterized by the active partner pushing and/or pulling and the passive partner being led or directed.

When this couple comes to my office for counseling, it's because she (the active partner) has initiated contact with me and has talked him (the passive partner) into coming "at least once to try it." In extreme cases, she issues an ultimatum. She is bursting at the seams with a well-rehearsed agenda for our time.

In marked contrast, the husband looks like the hunted, not the hunter. He figures that his wife has brought him to be "fixed up," and that it will be two (counselor and wife) against one. While he settles into a half-reclined position, she sits forward and immediately begins her laundry list of grievances.

Fifteen minutes into the interview, the husband still hasn't said anything. When he finally does speak she interrupts and/or corrects him, and when he doesn't talk she complains. Verbally, she is a skilled technician and he is a neophyte. When she takes him to task, he hangs his head, shaking it with a defeated look. I know he is thinking, "What's the use?"

Perhaps you're already taking sides. As you read the case of Tom and Susan, my educated guess is that you sided with Susan. How do I know? Because active partners are the ones who will read this book! You know what it feels like to live day to day with a nice, compliant, undependable, and unassertive person. You probably approach household chores thinking, "If I don't do this, it won't get done." For those chores he must do, you find yourself having to continually remind him. It's frustrating because he's undependable. At times you may catch yourself thinking, "He wasn't this way before we got married, and if I'd known he was going to be this way I would not have married him." Ironically, as I probe I usually find that in the beginning the husband's "go-along-for-the-ride" behavior was perceived as a "quiet strength" and a "likable, easygoing nature."

If you are an active partner, your feelings are very real and understandable. But be careful not to focus all the blame on him. I too am tempted to take your side, but I know from experience that both partners have contributed to the marital struggles. Taking sides in the "blame game" only reduces the chances for reconciliation. Instead, it's important to understand the characteristics of an Active-Passive marriage—how it begins, its inward and outward style, its strengths and weaknesses, and how to live with and adjust to your partner. You can learn to compensate for your weaknesses, build on your strengths, and move toward a more enjoyable and healthy marriage.

Beginnings

Most Active-Passive relationships start out complementary—filling each other's empty spaces. Tom and Susan were like that. When they met she was talkative and he was quiet, which meant he did not have to work as hard at the relationship. He was attentive because he had a physical drive and her energy and enthusiasm were attractive to him. She interpreted this attention as true involvement and concluded that he would and could be attentive in all areas. What she interpreted as quiet strength was actually his lack of confidence.

When there is anxiety in a relationship, men tend to become quiet and women tend to talk. Unchecked, it can get carried away. Susan had a natural concern to organize and establish the relationship. There was nothing unnatural about her drive; however, she overdid it. Over the years she became more and more active, making most of the decisions, while Tom conceded more and more of his vote to her. Now Susan interprets Tom's quietness, which used to be a strength, as desertion, while he thinks Susan wants to run him and maybe even the world.

Outward Style

In an Active-Passive marriage, outward behavior is dissimilar.

She appears to be her own person. If not formally employed, she usually works as a volunteer in activities such as church organist, Girl Scout leader, blood drive coordinator, Little League committee person, political worker, or Band Boosters fund drive chairperson. While she's on stage, the husband is part of the audience. Amazed and somewhat overwhelmed, he would like to ask her, "Why do you do all of this?" She would probably answer, "Someone has to do it, and you're sure not by sitting around or being gone."

The wife's competence extends into the home, and she usually handles the money, social arrangements, and church activities. She is the more active parent in listening, discipline, and support of the children. Through her drive, the children take advantage of such opportunities as music lessons, children's clubs, and athletic programs.

She does her best to keep her man on course as well, keeping his chore list full. He works steadily but, according to her, he could always improve. He shows up for meals but participates little in family talk. After supper he watches TV, retires to another room to read, or leaves to play ball. He believes he is not competent, capable, and adequate, like his wife. His impression is that she will never be satisfied. He remembers when he cleaned out the garage and how she pointed out all the things he missed. He thinks to himself, "So I missed something. Can't she appreciate what I did do?"

Friends and acquaintances may take sides. Some feel sorry for him because he has to put up with her overbearing manner. They would like to see him stand up and politely put her in her place. Others sympathize with her. "She has to do all the work," they think. "Why doesn't he try harder? I don't know how she puts up with him." If you do find yourself siding with one or the other, that may reflect your own relationship. Often it is easier for us to see our own situation in other marriages than to see it in ourselves.

Rarely does the couple sit and visit just for the fun of it. When they do talk, conversation is usually topical and safe. They are uncomfortable with discussion about their marriage, individual hopes and dreams, or personal victories or concerns. The children rarely see displays of affection between Mom and Dad, and are shocked or giggle with embarrassment if and when they do embrace. This couple has forgotten how to be lovers. Now they are doers—doers for their kids, families, friends, church, and employers. Love pats, winks, and mushy kisses are desired but also tension-producing.

Their physical relationship is only partially fulfilling. The wife's complaints about the sexual relationship are usually one or more of the following: He wants sex but doesn't do anything else in the marriage; he ignores sex altogether; she wants closeness, but her complaining drives him away. She may try to get results in the bedroom by initiating sex, or, if that does not work, she may turn off to sex herself, thinking, "If he is not going to take care of me, then I don't need to take care of him." In some cases her respect for him as a person may deteriorate to the point that sex becomes nauseating.

Meanwhile he finds it difficult to be sexually turned on by a person who is "on his case" all the time. He wants sex as much or more than his wife, but his feeling of being looked down upon throttles his natural drive to please her. Consequently, he shys away, waiting for cues from her as to when it is okay. Intercourse can be mechanical because they feel little freedom to "play" with or enjoy each another physically.

Inward Experience

Sometimes an Active-Passive couple feels helpless, as if the marriage is beyond both of them. But each suffers in his or her own private world, wanting it to be different but having no idea that the other person feels the same way. Attempts at improving the relationship are scary because neither wants to be hurt again. They resemble the military standoff of World War I with the Germans entrenched along one battle line and the Allies in trenches on the other side. Between them was "no-man's-land," and neither side dared advance toward the other. It is easy for this couple to stay in their own trenches because their fear of being hurt is more powerful than their confidence to deal honestly and openly with each other.

In highly developed, problem-plagued Active-Passive marriages, the wife will become angry. She has tried hard to make this marriage work but has received little cooperation. Expectations of what her man was going to do have floated away like helium-filled balloons. She feels he misled her and is upset that she fell for this guy.

Both parties feel they were gypped. He has to put up with a parental woman. She has to put up with a childish man. "If onlys" are a part of their mental dialogue: "If only she would quit putting me down"; "if only he would listen to me." They are imprisoned by their feelings, convinced that there is little they can do to change the situation.

Notice, despite the outward differences, their inward similarity. Underneath the surface the man and woman are very much alike in how they approach life. The diagram shows this inward similarity.

Active Partner	Passive Partner
Angry	Defeated
Victimized	Victimized
Dependent	Dependent

Each partner depends on the other for fulfillment and each is disappointed. They married to *get* rather than give. Their expectations are selfish: Her happiness depends upon his being capable and adequate; his happiness depends upon her being tolerant of his shortcomings.

This couple does not recognize how dependent they are on each other because the dependence is deeply rooted within them. Therefore they focus on outward differences. The more they look at each other's shortcomings, the more the symptoms increase. His quietness is not only a cause of her anger, but also an effect. Her demands cause his disinterest and his inattentiveness causes her needs.

I do not want to suggest that all Active-Passive marriages are tense. Many get along fairly well, and the reason they do is because the partners have come to the place in their personal growth where they are not so heavily dependent on each other. However, marital tension tends to fluctuate as one or both partners feels insecure and attempts to gain security in the spouse.

Strengths and Weaknesses

Most of us like to drink liquids either cold or hot—not lukewarm. Room-temperature Coke and lukewarm coffee leave a lot to be desired. In a sense the Active-Passive marriage personality is lukewarm. Like a pastel color, it doesn't shine brightly, nor is it totally dark and dull. This marriage doesn't attract much attention because so many of them exist.

The strengths and weaknesses of Active-Passive marriages are not extreme in most cases. These are average individuals in average marriages, living in average neighborhoods with average lifestyles. The important strengths are their persevering and stable nature. They are caring parents with a concern for their community. These couples tend to be loyal. They hang in there in marriage, job, and community. Sometimes their daily slice of life is not too exciting, but they come back the next day. They are proficient at living with the status quo.

As parents, they are not highly directive. They do not say, "You can do it, and here is how," or, "Watch me!" Instead, they say, "If you want to do something, we'll try to help." They are not neglectful, but neither are they out in front of their children showing them the way. They try their best to parent effectively with the personal resources available.

Their style of community cooperation is as willing participants rather than initiators or leaders. They respond to good causes, whether helping a sick neighbor, volunteering at the church, or giving to a special need.

Finally, these couples are dependable. They show up for work, band concerts, family get-togethers, and church activities. They are "Steady Toms" and "Stable Susans" who live according to predictable routines which include set meal times, paying all the bills each month, and always showing up at scheduled meetings.

While family structure is a strength, the family process is a significant weakness. Family process is the ability to effectively communicate and assertively deliver thoughts, feelings, and wants to others in the family. Their nemesis is fumbled communication rather than lack of communication. Abbreviated sentences, little or no eye contact, a raised or lowered voice, and avoidance of saying what one is really thinking describe the passive partner. He is in retreat, and the active partner is constantly frustrated with her passive husband. She cannot motivate him to tell her what he thinks, feels, or wants.

A common interaction might look something like this. Jane tells Dick that her parents have invited them for Sunday dinner in two weeks. Her question is simple: "Do you want to go?"

What Dick really wants to do is watch football on Sunday afternoon. Besides, he is uncomfortable at her parents' place because he feels like an outsider with dissimilar interests. But he thinks, "If I don't go, I'll never hear the end of it." So Dick answers, "Well, I guess that's okay if that's what you want to do." Not "yes" or "no" but "I guess so." Dick is indirectly telling Jane that he does not want to go and is at the same time shifting responsibility for the decision back to her. That way, if anything goes wrong, she is to blame.

In addition to an ineffective communication process, a second weakness in this couple is a subtle but ongoing feeling of inadequacy caused by comparing themselves to other couples. Among their acquaintances they can always see a better husband or a more understanding wife. When a person does not feel good about himself, it affects his confidence. And personal self-doubt undercuts confidence in dealing with a spouse. In the example of Dick and Jane, they maintain contact, but self-doubts limit their communication. Rather than learning to share their thoughts and feelings in a constructive and nondefensive way, they continue to tolerate fumbled communication.

When couples struggle with ineffective communication and feel inadequate, the natural result is a third weakness—evasive behavior. They avoid each other because they do not believe they are capable of pleasing each other. Look at Dick and Jane again. Dick is cleaning the garage, but thinking, "No matter how well I do this, Jane still complains. So the heck with it." Dick rushes the job, then goes inside disgusted. As he enters the house, Jane asks, "Do you want to have the Butlers over tonight?" "You decide," he snaps as he walks by her. "At least you could act interested!" she retorts. He ignores her comment and Jane is trapped. Does she go ahead and invite the Butlers, knowing that Dick will cooperate in a passive, sabotaging manner? Or does she confront him and give attention to his brush-off? She decides it's easier to make her plans and avoid the confrontation. Both are evasive. He avoids her because of previous put-downs and she ignores his intimidating silence.

Finally, from a clinical perspective, the major problem that exists to varying degrees in all Active-Passive marriages is dependency. Dependency is when one partner leans too much on the other to meet his or her individual needs. Usually this leaning occurs because when they married, they subconsciously expected their spouse to be all they needed them to be. Common sense suggests that this kind of unrealistic hope leads to trouble. Each partner, to a different extent, expects the other to meet his needs. Neither has accepted responsibility for his own life.

Improving the Marriage

It's important to remember each individual in the Active-Passive marriage entered the relationship with the best of intentions. The bottom line is that he or she cares for his mate and does not want to hurt him. He desires fulfillment in the marriage and wants the same for his spouse. There are many positive elements still at work between them, though they may be enduring significant disappointments, as the symptoms described in this chapter demonstrate. However, not all the symptoms described apply to all Active-Passive marriages.

Let's address the active partner first. Rather than complaining about what the passive partner has or has not done, she needs to give her spouse more compliments. She should also ask for his advice. This can open the door for the passive partner to feel like a competent person who is needed in the relationship. This may feel risky for the active partner who has lost confidence in her spouse. But it is important to give her partner room to develop and express his feelings in the decision-making process.

The active partner also assumes the risk of living in a relationship that will never be exactly what she would like. For example, a woman may believe that her husband should be the spiritual leader in the home. However, if he tends to be uninvolved and lacks initiative, she might work for months or years trying to get him to fulfill his "appropriate" role. But the more pressure she exerts, the more inadequate and passive he feels. It is my suggestion that she accept the reality of who he is, as an individual created by God. Go ahead and initiate some of the spiritual activity yourself, or just leave it alone for awhile. That is not to excuse his biblical responsibilities, but it does recognize his personality, and it allows God to change him as he realizes what God requires from him.

It is also important for the active partner to look at herself in the mirror and see how she presents herself to the family. She needs to realize that the general tone of attack or self-pity is not productive. It is important for the active partner to reduce her habit of blaming and complaining, regardless of the partner's behavior, because it will never motivate him to change.

Finally, I suggest that the active partner make a list of the positive elements of her marriage relationship. When she is disillusioned with the marriage, she tends to mentally rehearse what she doesn't like. She needs to change that pattern, following the instructions in Philippians 4:6-9, where Paul tells us to think about things that are good and righteous and pure. Paul goes on to say in verse 11 that he has learned to be content. I believe his contentness was at least partly the result of reminding himself of what was good and right instead of reviewing what was wrong.

The passive partner also faces a significant challenge. He needs to break through his natural tendency to avoid confrontation and learn to be more direct with his spouse. If this seems impossible, then he needs to take a course in assertiveness or obtain counsel and support from a close friend.

Let's take, for example, the husband whose wife criticizes the way he cleans the garage. In confronting his wife, Dick might say something like this: "Honey, I don't mind cleaning out the garage, but I don't want to hear complaints about how I clean it. If you choose to complain about it, you need to know that I will not clean out the garage. So either let me clean it my way, which I'll be glad to do, or if you want to complain, then you can clean it yourself or have it done by someone else."

It's important that this be said in an objective, caring way, without any hostility. Such directness will provide more strength to the passive partner and the marriage. This doesn't come naturally for him, so he must depend upon Christ for his strength.

What if the attempts by the active or passive partner are ignored? Remember that each person has a responsibility to act responsibly in a marriage relationship. This responsibility does not change whether a spouse responds to our attempts or not. Regardless of the response, a person often benefits in spiritual and personal growth as he or she attempts to act out his personal beliefs.

Attempts at improving and enriching this marriage by one or both parties will usually achieve positive results. The key is that both husband and wife learn to be less dependent on each other and more dependent on Christ. Jesus has made every provision for us to feel accepted, loved, and fulfilled in our relationships. As we learn to allow Him to be the source of our happiness and peace, we will be freed from overdependence on the behavior of our spouse.

The Active-Passive Marriage

	Behavior	Feelings
Active	Pushing/pulling the other	Victimized, taken advantage of
Passive	Avoiding and withdrawing	Victimized, taken advantage of

Theme—Leaning
Major Problem—Dependency
Secondary Problem—Family of Origin
Major Strength—Stability

CHAPTER 5

The Active-Resistant Marriage

I first met Jan and Ken at our city's annual charity ball. She was dressed in a full-length gown, he in a black tuxedo. Instantly I was drawn to Jan because of her vivacious, outgoing personality. She seemed to radiate self-confidence and drew my wife and me into easy conversation. She seemed particularly proud to tell us that she was a homemaker with two small children. On this night she was to receive an honorary award for her many hours of volunteer work.

Ken was not quite so outgoing. He was a successful businessman, and it was obvious that he had many friends and acquaintances. It didn't take long to realize that he had a keen wit which was often directed at his smiling wife. Everyone in the group enjoyed this couple and they were the center of much attention. Both were socially poised individuals who seemed to have it all together.

That's why it was a shock when, one week later, Jan was in my office asking for help. In the public eye, this couple looked great. Their struggle for intimacy was a private one, unnoticed by all except perhaps their closest friends. All of their social charm did not extend behind closed doors. They are a classic example of an Active-Resistant couple.

Ken and Jan met in college and were college sweethearts. In her eyes, he was a "great big senior" and to him, she was a "cute little sophomore cheerleader." Jan was flattered that an older guy would choose her and liked the fact that he was from a good family and seemed somewhat religious. And he enjoyed the fact that she was fun, attractive, and very popular.

Jan was a hard worker and goal-oriented. Her parents had sacrificed in order to equip her as an individual, and she had taken full advantage of this to win several honors and become socially graceful and in tune with many areas of life. However, she lacked self-assurance and constantly felt the need to accomplish more in order to gain approval. She couldn't stand the thought of rejection for her actions or skills. Of course, no one knew that she had these feelings of self-doubt because on the surface she remained polished and confident.

Ken's dad was a blue-collar worker and his mother a warm person who was very involved in her church. His mother and older sisters spoiled him, and in school his natural talent made him a leader, even though he was not a highly directed individual.

As soon as Jan and Ken married they moved to another city, where Ken enrolled in law school. He enjoyed his chosen career and quickly developed close friends with whom he spent a great deal of time. Jan agreed to work because money was scarce but soon began to resent the time Ken was spending with his friends studying and seemingly taking life easy. In addition to her job, she had to cook and clean while he took no initiative to help around the apartment. That seemed unfair to her, and she did not hesitate to tell him so. Being intimidated by Jan's faultfinding, Ken tried to ignore it at first, then chose to laugh it off with sarcastic humor. Over the next few months, however, she became more and more critical of Ken's attitude. Hoping to avoid further conflict, Ken began to lie to Jan about what he was doing. He didn't really want to lie, but neither did he want to hurt Jan. He simply decided that what she didn't know wouldn't hurt her.

After Ken's graduation, they moved to a small town and Ken set up his law practice. It wasn't long before Ken realized that the town was too small and that perhaps the city would provide more opportunity for developing a large practice. Jan backed him and even helped out by doing his accounting and decorating his new office. She also enjoyed the larger city, finding it a great place to expand her opportunities and abilities.

At first, setting up a new practice caused some monetary strain. During this tight-money time, Jan not only felt anxious but also frustrated with Ken. Often he chose to go to the men's club instead of making business calls. Jan was again quick to tell him how she felt, and was dismayed when Ken tartly informed her that she was his wife and only his wife, and that he could take care of "his" business. Ken also felt that he should not talk to Jan about business situations because they only caused her to worry and yell at him.

Soon after their move, their first daughter was born. Jan enjoyed this new little life and began to invest most of her time with their firstborn. This was very satisfying to Jan, but unfortunately it began to separate her from Ken. Because she was continually tired, she quit her job, but that strapped them financially. Jan noticed that when they went out together, they would still talk, but there was no sense of connection. They would discuss general topics, such as business, friends, or their children, but when they tried to talk freely with each other, Jan felt an emptiness.

Ken continued to monitor comments about his business or his work, having learned that Jan was always ready to give him unsolicited advice. If he disagreed, an argument followed. Unfortunately, Ken never experienced arguments in his home, so they made him extremely uncomfortable. He felt overwhelmed while arguing with Jan and inept at defending his own viewpoint.

As the children grew, Jan became more and more oriented around her kids and their activities. Ken, on the other hand, spent his free time at the golf club, playing cards, or in local politics. He spent very little time at home and didn't care to hear what was going on, preferring instead to retreat in silence or simply walk away from his angry, frustrated wife. To him, his reward for trying to do his best was a wife who was always on his case.

For Jan, though, her reward for trying to be the best mother she could was rejection. She felt she had received a raw deal in this marriage. Although she was angry, she was also lonely and sad. The more she experienced feelings of hurt and pain, the more her self-doubt increased. She tried to compensate for those feelings by busying herself in community volunteer work.

In many ways it seems ironic that Ken and Jan chose each other. Jan did not feel she deserved to be accepted for who she was. So she married someone who did not do a good job of demonstrating affection or approval. Ken did not feel adequate in handling interpersonal contact, so he married someone who could. Unfortunately, Jan reminded him continually of his inadequacy. Instead of dealing with his feelings of failure, he retreated while flinging verbal barbs at his wife. Ironically, both chose someone who could compensate for their felt internal weakness, though they didn't realize it.

The Active-Resistant couple present themselves as sharp, capable individuals, able to carry on easy conversations and handle themselves well socially. Others see them as fun-loving and enjoyable to be around. Often they are the life of a party. However, it is not uncommon for them to part in social situations—each going his own way. When they are together, they tend to keep their distance with "fun-loving" jokes or some mild form of sarcasm. They, as well as others around them, laugh off the "jabs," but underneath the laughter the hurt can be devastating.

The Active-Resistant roles are populated by both sexes. However, the man is more often the resistant partner and the woman the active partner. Many times these marriages are made up of talented professional individuals with strong opinions and values, and the marriage is characterized by competition. With the increasing number of professional women in the work force, the number of Active-Resistant marriages has also increased. For purposes of illustration, I am identifying the woman as the active spouse and the man as the resistant partner.

As we examine this marriage, you'll notice many similarities with the Active-Passive personality. But it is important to note the differences also. The Active-Passive marriage tends to be more socially cautious while the Active-Resistant one is socially involved and works as a team while "on stage." You'll find that the Active-Passives tend to be more compliant, easygoing, and cooperative while the Active-Resistants are assertive and individual thinkers. Active-Passives want to know the rules while the Active-Resistants question the rules. When struggling, the Active-Passive is like a "cold war," with silence, unfinished discussions, and lingering issues. The Active-Resistants usually have a "hot" war, with stubborn, verbal bouts and each partner wanting the last word.

Beginnings

This couple is attracted to each other by their strengths and apparent confidence. Each is an individual who seems to have it all together. Each likes being around people who are somewhat assertive, aggressive, and forward-moving. Their friends know what they want to do in life, and they have opinions about everything from politics to religion. While each is comfortable in groups, the active one is usually more socially adept and skilled than the resistant partner. Often it is the active partner's social electricity that initially attracts the resistant partner.

This couple has a history of accomplishing their short-term goals. In fact, when they decide to become engaged, they often don't marry right away because each wants to finish his own personal projects, such as school or special training or saving a certain amount of money. Often they're in their midtwenties when they do marry, having dated from one to three years or even longer.

Feelings of love and physical attraction for each other usually serve as a temporary cover for a serious problem. If you were to interview their parents and friends, you would probably discover that both the man and the woman could be accused of being stubborn and self-willed. They have developed a lifelong habit of wanting things their own way and believing that their way is always best. But in the excitement of their high-profile relationship, friends ignore that tendency and are excited about this couple's future.

Outward Style

The theme of the Active-Resistant marriage is temperature. Usually the active partner is accused of being overly emotional and sensitive. She continually wants the relationship heated up. She wants to be noticed and complimented and to have her husband act like he enjoys her company. On the other hand, the resistant one is charged with being emotionally distant and cold. She doesn't want to turn down the thermostat. He thinks, "It's warm enough already, and if it gets any hotter, I'll melt."

Over and over the active partner attempts to promote closeness in the relationship, only to get little or no response from the resistant partner. He projects a noninvolved, disinterested, almost placid stance. In effect he keeps the active one on edge because she never quite knows where she stands with her uncommunicative husband. His standard reply to her "How do I look?" question is met with a mumbled "Okay." If she asks, "Honey, do you love me?" he nonchalantly answers, "Of course."

His basic personality is marked by a logical, cognitive approach to life. Because he is often professional, he is used to making decisions that affect other people's lives or that involve large amounts of money. He considers himself good at just about anything he chooses to undertake and could be classified as a perfectionist. That's one reason it's hard for him to accept the failure he feels in his marriage. It is difficult, if not impossible, to tell a perfectionist that he is not perfect.

The goal for the active person in this relationship is to experience some heartfelt communication. She continually seeks to put life into the relationship and desperately wants him to pay attention to her. Unfortunately, she often chooses complaining and "pity parties" as an avenue to secure his affection. He chooses to resist her subtle attempts for closeness. In fact, the more she complains, the more he moves in the opposite direction. He immerses himself in his work, hobby, volunteer activities, or even an affair.

Sometimes the only way he knows how to show he cares is by buying things for his wife. In fact, he prides himself on this ability. Unfortunately, these attempts do not satisfy her need for closeness.

When Jan and I discussed this particular aspect of the Active-Resistant relationship, she recalled her anger when Ken bought her a new car for her birthday. She thought it ironic that he would give her anything at all, since they had not even spoken to each other for two weeks. Needless to say, she was as confused by his attempt to please her as he was at her anger over the surprise gift.

Many times the resistant husband sees his wife's demands as an avalanche—the snow careening down the mountainside, overwhelming everything in its pathway. Just as most people would do anything to avoid an avalanche, he does whatever he can to stay out of her way. He unconsciously fears that he'll be lost in the flood of her demands, so he resists at all costs. He firmly believes that if he cooperates with her just a little, she will only want more and he will never be able to satisfy all her demands. He doesn't retreat like a whipped puppy; he just resists.

The wife has a legitimate need for attention, recognition, and closeness. Unfortunately, the more she wants to be close, the more he tends to resist. The more he resists, the more attention she craves, and the cycle continues unbroken.

At this point it is not uncommon for the active wife to be hurt and confused by her husband. Often she blames herself for being inadequate, unattractive, or unappealing. She may attempt to lure him into closeness with sexual advances, a new hairdo, community accomplishments, or anything she believes is important to him. In Jan's case, she found herself ignoring her own personal preference and dressing exactly the way Ken wanted her to dress. But he rarely cooperated with the compliments she desired, which made her angry for stooping so low.

Through all of this, the woman's emotions are playing volleyball, bouncing back and forth between hurt feelings and anger because of his insensitivity—an insensitivity that only seems apparent in their relationship. Over the years she can become hostile toward her husband, but she often covers it up with layers of denial. Sometimes she will try to distance herself from him, either by not speaking to him or by complete avoidance for a day, a week, or perhaps even a month. Then, when she can no longer stand the loneliness, she returns to try again. It is extremely difficult for her to accept the fact that she is unloved.

The outward style of the Active-Resistant relationship covers a wide range from healthy to unhealthy. As you can see, the behavior of either party affects the relationship.

	Active Partner	Resistant Partner
Healthy	Assertive	Controlled
Healthy	Correcting, Complaining	Reserved
Healthy	Accusing	Cool
Unhealthy	Demanding	Hardened

Inward Experience

Internally both partners are trapped in feelings of loneliness, caution, and confusion. Each can handle most things in life, but neither has figured out how to deal with the spouse. Because they are determined individuals, they bury their confusion and pretend that nothing is bothering them. The morning after a disheartening encounter, they may sit at the breakfast table carrying on a polite conversation. Both know they are bothered, and they know their partner knows they are bothered, but both are too stubborn to talk it through. They are lonely people who need to bridge the gap, but their pride won't allow them to.

When I visit with these people on an individual basis, each will tell me of the partner's lack of appreciation. Each has persuaded himself that he is a good person, thinking, "I get applause and credit from work, my friends, and my church peers—I must not be all bad." When the couple does try to affirm each other and share their feelings, it often ends in misunderstanding.

The active partner, usually the woman, came into the relationship wanting love, affirmation, and affection, yet felt undeserving of it. She believes she has to earn love and doesn't believe she can be loved just for who she is. Over and over she tries to prove herself to him, hoping and praying that somehow he'll respond.

Afraid of being engulfed and trapped, the resistant partner backs away, believing that by loving her he will not be able to fulfill his own needs. He never doubts that she wants everything he has to give, and thinking that this still won't please her, he decides to not even try.

When an Active-Resistant marriage starts having problems, both partners often feel some anger and guilt. They are angry not only at each other but also at themselves for participating in a futile endeavor. They realize that their problems are not unilateral; each has some responsibility for the success and failure of their relationship, so each has a sense of self-blame. This guilt often becomes so painful that they angrily blame the other partner.

As this guilt, anger, and even depression builds, behavior begins to be conditioned by the partner. The marital cesspool stagnates their ability to be responsible for self. In addition, they begin to believe that the behavior of the spouse is intentional and premeditated rather than a reflection of individual personality. For example, the resistant partner resists for self-protection, but she perceives his resistance as rejection.

The more the active partner feels rejected and unloved, the more she becomes aware of her need for intimacy and closeness. Intimacy, or the desire for it, becomes the focus of her life. Often this craving moves into fantasy as she begins to expect more than is found in most marriages. The halfhearted or minimal attempts by her husband to promote closeness are rejected because they fall far short of what she has convinced herself she needs and deserves.

The resistant partner believes that love means taking care of his wife by giving, providing, and accomplishing. She rejects his way of showing love, and he rejects what she says she needs, knowing that it is extreme. So both feel rejected.

Strengths and Weaknesses

There is no question that this couple has many fine attributes. They know how to have fun. They're active, involved, and proficient workers. They usually do well earning, budgeting, and giving money. The church, the community, and their children profit from their expertise and competence. Leadership and initiative are natural to them. They make decisions and follow through with those decisions. You can see why these people are sought by others.

This couple is usually fairly direct with each other. They might not like what they hear from their partner, but at least they don't wonder what the other person thinks about a particular issue. That directness is limited, however, because each finds it difficult to talk about inner feelings.

Their children soak up the competence, individuality, decisiveness, and responsibility displayed by Mom and Dad. These kids receive attention and expert guidance, and as a result they believe in themselves. However, they find themselves sandwiched between Mom and Dad when the parents do not get along. The kids admire their parents' skills but are hurt and offended by their parents' conflict.

The strengths of the Active-Resistant are centered around the strengths of each individual. Ironically, those individual strengths contribute to their most glaring weakness. How do you get two strong and often stubborn-independent people to work together in caring harmony? It's like trying to mix oil with water. Consequently, this couple tends to compete, which leads to tension and sets up their struggle with closeness and intimacy.

Fear of disapproval and/or failure motivates these two individuals to work hard. However, this same fear creates havoc in their marriage relationship. Trust is one of their major weaknesses. They simply do not believe that their spouse will love and accept them if their personal weaknesses are known. They are extremely cautious about displaying or discussing any weakness or need for fear that the other partner may take advantage of them. They believe they must somehow prove themselves while protecting themselves from each other.

Unfortunately, this creates an unending cycle. The active partner works harder and harder, hoping somehow to get recognized by her husband. Her pushing forces him to resist, causing her to feel abandoned and rejected, which is her greatest fear. She doesn't realize that she is actually sabotaging the closeness she so desperately craves by reminding her husband of his shortcomings. He then sabotages any closeness he needs by pointing out her faults or defending his behavior.

Both partners have a deep need to feel worthwhile. She feels a sense of accomplishment when she is appreciated, recognized, and supported on an interpersonal level. He feels self-respect when he accomplishes on a professional, vocational level. Each, in the drive to feel worthwhile, roadblocks the other person. He does not cooperate in fulfilling her need for closeness because he thinks that will hinder his need for professional growth. She in turn rejects his form of love (gift-giving, material provisions) because she feels bought off while her deepest needs continue unmet.

This couple tends to always remain the same distance apart. When she moves toward him, he takes one step back. If she takes one step back, he feels the freedom to come a little closer. It's like they are holding hands, but at arms' length. They are connected, but they are afraid of losing their own identity to the other person. Somehow they never learned how to be close to another person. To them, closeness means they must lose part of who they are, and that causes too much anxiety. So instead they back away.

Why Do They Struggle with Closeness?

The family-of-origin experience is likely the major contributing factor to the closeness/intimacy problem. Although they are probably not aware of it, this man and woman are working out unresolved difficulties they had as children. Some marriage therapists have suggested that marriage is the process of putting closure on the unfinished business of our family of origin. In other words, our parents and siblings so affect us that we often choose marriage partners in an attempt to compensate for what we did not receive in childhood.

Active-Resistant partners approach family life differently. The active partner questions her worth. As a child she was involved in many activities and developed the idea that her parents loved her more if she performed well and loved her less if she was bad. Sometimes, at a young age, one or both parents may have minimally supported her. This experience intensified her need to feel secure and appreciated. She developed an unconscious attitude that she cannot be accepted by anyone because Mom or Dad, or both, did not accept her. This feeling of rejection by a parent runs so deeply that the active partner, while desiring closeness, does not expect it and in fact may sabotage it. She will nag her husband about closeness, but by nagging will guarantee distance. She lives in chronic fear of rejection but doesn't know how to prevent it.

The resistant partner has a family heritage that emphasized rightness above closeness. One or both parents were often overprotective or overinvasive, and he feels that his boundaries as a person have been offended. He resents any "hovering" or crowding because his family smothered him.

Improving the Marriage

Considerable stability can be established when the active partner modifies her striving for closeness. If she will redirect her energies in some other activities, it may remove the pressure felt by the resistant partner. This will allow him to reenter the relationship. When the resistant partner feels room to breathe, closeness becomes more appealing.

It may seem unfair to suggest that adjustments start with the active partner. In reality, though, that is the best place to

begin. It is simply a fact that the active partner is more motivated and aware of the relationship and therefore more capable of initiating adjustments.

The active partner can help the resistant partner by doing
such things as curtailing phone calls, suggesting that he stay
at work or go back to work if he needs to, or being gone (at
a meeting or shopping) when he gets home. The gap she creates
gives him room to enter the relationship.

Also, it is imperative that she retrain her mind to accept that
his providing behavior is his way of showing love. She must
let him love her in that way instead of allowing herself to think
she is being bought off.

Finally, she must confront her fear that if she does back off
on her demand for attention and accepts his "payoffs," he will
never do anything more than just provide for her. She's afraid
he'll *never* want to get close to her, that he'll think that what
he is doing is sufficient. That's a risk she takes, but obviously
her attempts to persuade him haven't worked. Usually, given
enough time, the resistant partner's need for closeness draws
him back to her.

Likewise, the resistant partner needs to confront a fear that
his wife will demand marathon feeling-oriented discussions,
and be offended if he does anything on his own. His fear is
unfounded. Yes, she would like attention, but she doesn't need
large doses. As far as having him around all the time, he would
get in her way. But she would feel good if he displayed interest
in being with her.

A major challenge for both partners is to risk telling each
other how they feel. A few simple changes can close that gap.
Instead of accusations and sarcasm, the resistant one could
walk up to his spouse and compliment her. When giving the
compliment he should maintain eye contact, smile, and give
her a hug. Initially the active partner may be suspicious. She
may ask, "Why are you telling me that?" "What do you want?"
"What do you have up your sleeve?" But if he listens without
reacting, she will soon begin to realize that he is genuinely
interested in her.

The active partner also needs to be brave and make a
statement like, "You know, sometimes I pick on you because
I want so much from you. I do care for you, but I realize that
part of what I want is only for me, not for you. That's unfair,

and I want you to know that I'm beginning to realize that, in your own way, you're doing the best you can to show me that you care." When the active partner tells her husband that she has expected too much from him, it often frees him up to be closer to her.

This couple needs to realize that their most significant strength—individuality—can easily become their biggest weakness. Their greatest help will come when each chooses to place himself as raw clay on the turning spindle of the Master Craftsman. The apostle Paul expressed it best in Philippians 2:3-8:

> Do nothing from selfishness or empty conceit, but with humility of mind let each of you regard one another as more important than himself; do not merely look out for your own personal interests, but also for the interests of others. Have this attitude in yourselves which was also in Christ Jesus, who, although He existed in the form of God, did not regard equality with God a thing to be grasped, but emptied Himself, taking the form of a bond-servant, and being made in the likeness of men. And being found in appearance as a man, He humbled Himself by becoming obedient to the point of death, even death on a cross.

When these two capable people choose to submit to God, significant progress can be made in the relationship. This does not mean that they lose their will, but rather that they are choosing to put themselves under the direction of the Lord Himself. This passage declares that true selfhood is realized when an individual allows Christ to give him the power to be a servant to someone else.

This same concept appears in Matthew 20:26-28. In the preceding verses James and John had desired a prominent position in Jesus' kingdom. Christ's response was: "Whoever wishes to become great among you shall be your servant, and whoever wishes to be first among you shall be your slave; just as the Son of Man did not come to be served, but to serve, and to give His life a ransom for many." Jesus declared His strength by becoming a great servant. Likewise, the invitation to this couple is to be the best at what Jesus prescribed—being a servant.

The Active-Resistant Marriage

	Behavior	**Feelings**
Active	Manipulating closeness	Unloved/wants love
	Independent	Optimistic
Resistant	Keeping partner at arms' length; independent	Smothered, crowded, afraid of love, confident

Theme—Lack of Intimacy
Major Problem—Self-Orientation
Secondary Problem—Family of Origin
Major Strength—Individual Competence

CHAPTER 6

The Helper-Helpee Marriage

The Helper-Helpee marriage is a relationship of contrasts. It began because one person had a problem and the other was available to help, and it is sustained by one or the other having to meet a major ongoing need in the partner's life. Bob and Karen are perfect examples.

Karen was a junior at the university when she met Bob, who had transferred there as a second-semester freshman. She was 20; he was 21. Three years before, lack of money, problems at home, a few misdemeanors, and poor grades had caused Bob to join the Army. Military life helped him get a handle on things, and now getting an education was Bob's goal. Karen was an excellent student, but she struggled with feelings of social inadequacy. A dating relationship with another student had recently gone sour and she was crushed—so much so that she stopped taking care of herself. Her hair was a mess and her clothing unkempt.

Five weeks into the semester their respective dorms had an exchange party. Bob and Karen each went alone and ended up sitting at the same table. Bob was not timid, so he introduced himself to Karen and the others. Karen was immediately attracted to him. His black hair and dark brown eyes accompanied a kind and strong countenance. Later, when Karen asked him about his classes, Bob admitted his struggles in English. His writing skills left much to be desired. Karen offered to help and he gladly accepted.

Karen could hardly contain herself as she prepared for the first "tutoring" session. She put on her favorite outfit and set her hair perfectly. They met at the library, and as they talked Karen discovered that Bob had some learning disabilities that had gone undetected until the latter part of high school. He was intelligent but still needed special help.

Afterward they went out for a Coke, and Karen told Bob about her recent break-up. Bob listened and encouraged her, pointing out her strengths. He didn't seem like so many other guys, looking out for themselves. He was genuine and directed, and Karen was impressed. Bob liked her too. He respected her intelligence, sensitivity, and good looks.

The rest of the year, they helped each another and their friendship led to a more serious relationship. However, there were problems. He felt like she had to have him around, and occasionally it was more of an obligation to be with her than a desire. She became nervous when he was with other women from his classes. She knew she should not be jealous, but she was. When she admitted her fears to him, he felt sorry for her. After all, she had done a lot for him; he might not have done so well in school without her help.

Karen was very thankful to Bob. He not only helped her get out of a rut, but he believed in her. Karen felt dependent upon Bob and did not want anything to disrupt the relationship, so she covered reactions that she thought might upset him. But she was not totally at ease in the relationship. Sometimes she felt like his project rather than his equal. She was secure, like a peasant with the king, but how do a peasant and a king have an intimate relationship?

Bob and Karen were married after she graduated. Bob still had two years of school, so she worked while he completed his education. She helped him complete school assignments and he listened to her frustrations about work. Gradually Bob began to feel like he had a child on his hands. Karen needed constant reassurance, and it seemed like she dealt with very few things on her own. He started losing respect for her but wouldn't tell her so because he didn't want to hurt her. Since he could not be truthful about his feelings, he tried to put them aside, hoping that someday the relationship would improve.

Karen confided to a close friend that Bob was like a father. She liked his caring and take-charge spirit. However, she did not take kindly to being treated like a child, though she had to admit that she felt better when he was around. She expected Bob to respond to her needs—after all, she was always ready to help him out—and felt some anger when he acted as if he didn't care. There were many times that she believed he got his way by ignoring her, not even asking for her opinion. It was as if she was the one doing all the adjusting. She felt trapped between needing him and resenting him.

Over the years, with two children and three moves, Bob lost his energy and motivation to help Karen. He was tired of "pumping her up." He felt guilty for failing to help her and angry at her for failing to improve. One weekend he finally told her how he really felt, and she crumbled. She was upset, hurt, and frantic. Karen assured him that she would get better. Over the weeks she did make strides, but Bob did not acknowledge them. Then Karen began to think about all the times she had given in to him and tried to cooperate: "This is the thanks I get for all my work, the moves, and the children."

Karen's anger began to come out. As she laid into Bob, he thought to himself, "If I tell her how I feel, she gets upset and can't handle it, but if I keep it to myself I get frustrated. It would be easier to get out of this whole mess." But Bob didn't really want to terminate the marriage, since he didn't believe in divorce. She had done her part, and he felt sorry for her, but he knew they needed help.

• • •

There are many Bob-and-Karen-type marriages, in which one or both of the partners has an ongoing problem that nips at their heels like an overzealous neighborhood hound. The malady comes in many forms. He is 43; she is 25. He is black; she is white. She has an MBA; he runs a garage. She attended prep schools; he doesn't know what purpose is served by the smaller fork in a dinner setting.

About 8 to 10 percent of American marriages fall into this personality. In addition, this personality is often a secondary trait to another marriage personality, such as Active-Passive or Active-Resistant. When you get together with a Helper-Helpee couple, you often feel this is a mismatch. Debbie is from the city and appreciates classical music. Dudley grew up in a less sophisticated environment and has never attended a symphony concert. What are some of the challenges they might encounter? She wants a Florentine lamp; he would be satisfied with the $8.99 special. She wants to attend the opera;

he prefers a country-western concert. She follows *Dress for Success*; Levi's are fine for him. She orders chicken cordon bleu at a formal restaurant; he prefers a hamburger at McDonald's.

Just what does Debbie see in Dudley? She probably sees a project—someone who needs "fixing up." They're getting along depends upon Dudley improving. Remember the story of Cinderella? When the prince discovered that Cinderella's foot fit the slipper, he was elated. When they married, did they move into his castle or to her humble dwelling with her wicked sisters? The castle, of course. Cinderella was the one who had to adapt to new surroundings. She had to change, not the prince; he was already royalty. That sounds simple enough in a fairy tale, but in real life it's not quite so easy.

Back to Debbie and Dudley. When they are in a social setting, each is very aware of the other's presence. Debbie is thinking, "I wonder how he's doing? He seemed pretty nervous about this reception. I get so tired of being concerned about him; I'm going to have a good time regardless." He is thinking, "She's probably wondering how I'm doing," and/or, "She is ignoring me and it doesn't seem to bother her."

The difference between Debbie and Dudley suggests that one of them is a caretaker (Debbie) and the other one is taken care of (Dudley). Their friends tend to ask Debbie how Dudley is doing. Those friends also believe that Dudley is the one who needs to get his act together, which reinforces her "togetherness" and his limitations. It is difficult for the couple and their friends to abandon the idea that the marriage problem is the helpee's and that if the helpee changed, the relationship would improve.

I'm a little nervous when I work with a Debbie and Dudley in marital therapy. They are often so unequal that to accomplish some form of compatibility is a tall order. Not all Helper-Helpee marriages end up in counseling, but when they do, I buckle up for a rough ride. But compatibility is possible if both partners are willing to work. First they need to understand the dynamics of their relationship. So we'll examine that, then look at some ways to improve the marriage.

Beginnings

Books and movies abound with stories that have a rescue

theme. Someone in need is rescued by the "good guy." The knight in shining armor comes to the rescue of the maiden in distress. In my youth, Roy Rogers and Dale Evans always came through in the nick of time. More recently, Luke Skywalker saves his people from oppression. Helper-Helpee marriages exude the theme of rescue. The helper (savior) rescues someone (helpee) in distress. The saving begins in the premarital relationship and continues as a pattern throughout the marriage.

Take, for example, Sandra, who was having a tough time with her parents. She moved to a large suburban area to find work. No matter what she did for them, her parents barely responded. Cookies, trips home, and calls went begging for appreciation. Naturally, Sandra felt rejected and despondent.

In addition, she was having some health problems. Ray, an older, single coworker, noticed that Sandra was not her normal, cheerful self. At a lunch break he asked her, "Say, what's going on—something bugging you?"

Sandra was caught off-guard, and her emotions took over. Two tears trickled down her cheeks. "I'm sorry for crying. It's nothing."

"Come on, tell me about it," Ray said as he leaned forward, his elbow on the table and cheek resting in his hand.

He looks like he really cares, she thought to herself. So she told him what was bothering her. In the following weeks, Ray helped her see things from a different vantage point, insisted that she see a doctor, and even put a few "bucks in the till" to pull her through financially. They became closer and closer friends, and finally decided to marry.

If Sandra had not had a problem and Ray had not pitied her, the relationship would probably never have started. Now that it has, a style also has begun. Ray, the savior, is to take care of Sandra. He expects to give, she expects to take. But too much of that will not be good for their marriage.

It's a similar story for most Helper-Helpee marriages. The couple begins their relationship by dealing with their parents or difficulties like depression, anxiety, failing school, poor vocational performance, social inadequacies, poor self-concept, or poor financial management. Their relationship is centered around one person helping the other who is in need. Often the couple misinterprets this helping relationship as romance.

While this couple feels good about each other, they are also somewhat indebted for the help, and that feeling of indebtedness binds them. They do not feel particularly romantic because part of their attraction is due to feeling sorry for the other person. However, they continue the relationship because neither wants to hurt the other.

Outward Style

This may seem harsh, but generally speaking, participants in the Helper-Helpee marriage are givers and takers. Both are using the other person to meet their own needs. The helper gains fulfillment by taking a helping role and the helpee meets his personal needs by being a receiver from his partner. I believe these thoughts and beliefs are mostly subconscious, so before this couple can change, they must realize that they have an exaggerated focus on themselves. They are more interested in pleasing themselves than in meeting the needs of others.

The external contracts can take a variety of forms. One may be a "doctor," the other a "patient." One is a "counselor," the other a "counselee." One is a "socialite," the other a "social trainee." No matter what the particular arrangement, the characteristic of the marriage is that one partner is in charge of the other.

The problem-theme orientation is kept alive when the helper says things like "How are you feeling today?" or "Be sure and take your pills" or "I filled out that job application for you." The helpee feels trapped between "Who does he think he is? I can do it myself" and "I don't know what I would do without him."

Another wrinkle in some of these marriages is the reciprocal arrangement, in which partners take turns being the helper. The roles may reverse every few months or may last several years. Even though they shift roles—each taking turns as the helper—the basic dynamic of the marriage stays the same: orientation around a problem and someone coming to the rescue.

Jim and Renee are a perfect example. Jim was a salesman but had a serious kidney problem. His wife struggled with depression and anxiety that occasionally required hospitalization. Jim had his best months in sales when Renee was emotionally slumped. However, when his kidneys acted up, she immediately improved. Her depression and anxiety vanished as she took charge of the family.

Inward Experience

It is wearing to have to deal with the same problem over a long period of time. Helpers and helpees know what that feels like. They get tired of dealing with the same issue or issues over and over again. At times they feel exasperated, not necessarily about the whole marriage, but with regard to their "difficult" area. The helper is tired of helping and the helpee is tired of being helped. It is like a leg chain for prisoners: They are not immobilized, but they definitely are slowed down, and they always know it's there.

Two common emotions for this couple are anger and guilt—anger because they are frustrated and guilt because they think they should do a better job. In our example of Bob and Karen, she was angry because she subconsciously thought Bob should have done a better job of assisting her. She may even have wondered why Bob could not generate some new, creative ways to come to her aid. Bob was angry too. He was upset with himself for not doing a better job and upset with Karen for not trying harder and standing on her own without needing him so much.

The anger leads to guilt feelings. For example, Bob felt guilty because Karen still had a problem; he felt it was his fault for not being a better helper. Karen felt guilty for not doing better. She reasoned that Bob's help was more than sufficient, and therefore it was her fault for not improving. Note that neither Bob nor Karen felt true guilt, since they had not done anything wrong. Rather, they were uncomfortable with themselves because their efforts were not successful.

By feeling angry and guilty, the partners avoid self-examination. If each were to examine his own motivation, he would discover selfishness. The helper's self-worth is measured by his successes in the lives of other people. This "savior" works very hard at picking up people who are in need. Often he is threatened by people who are of equal stature, so he takes on individuals whom he considers of less ability and adequacy. His desire to be a caretaker is often motivated by the desire to feel good about himself rather than by helping others.

The helpee is also selfish. She spends a large portion of her life focusing on self-improvement. In some ways she likes nothing better than to have a helper available as a constant companion and counselor. At other times she is offended by the helper because she knows that, in order to really be healthy, she needs to solve her own problem.

As ridiculous as it may sound, both partners subconsciously recognize that in order for the marriage to survive, there must be a problem. In extreme cases they will even cooperate in maintaining a problem or creating a new problem.

For example, the helper can actually sabotage the helpee's improvement by continually focusing on the helpee's short-comings. The helpee, on the other hand, keeps the cycle going by being resistant or noncompliant.

In the midst of this melee, each partner ends up blaming the other for the difficulty of the marriage relationship. Neither of them likes the role, but they don't know what to do about it. The relationship does not result in growth for either person. In fact, growth is a threat.

Strengths and Weaknesses

One significant strength of the Helper-Helpee marriage is empathy. Even though neither partner likes the problem focus of the marriage, each does display an ability to understand. Obviously, this empathy is taken to the extreme. But that ability is important to the health of any marriage relationship.

Another good thing about this marriage is that each partner wants to improve as a person. Each wants to make personal and spiritual progress, but can't figure out how to do it.

Continual focus on problems is the major weakness of the Helper-Helpee marriage. Part of what contributes to their difficulty is inability to equalize the relationship. For example, how does a person who is 15 years older than his spouse ever become the same age? Obviously that's not possible. Those built-in differences tend to keep a couple separated more than they want to be.

Improving the Marriage

Significant improvement will begin to take place in this marriage when the two people move away from the focus on their problems. To make that shift, it is essential that they start relating to each other in an upbeat, progressive, and goal-oriented way.

Also, the helper must stop helping the helpee little by little. In order to facilitate this, he may need to channel his helping energies in another direction, such as his local church or Boy Scout club. The more he stops being his wife's "caretaker" or "counselor," the more she is able to take responsibility for her own personal improvement. It's the same idea as a parent helping a child learn to function independently.

It is important for the helpee to not overreact when this happens. She may be angry because she feels he is abandoning her, but she needs to recognize this as an opportunity to develop as an individual. The helpee, to bring significant improvement in the relationship, must take some risks. It is a risk to live without the security of her helper in that problem area.

To make the transition, she might consider having a spiritually mature person disciple her. This will help her learn how to go to God for strength to overcome her weakness. She will gain an increased sense of personal identity as she places her security in God. And she will realize that God can help her develop strength in any area where she lacks confidence.

As the relationship matures, this couple has the potential to help other couples work through their differences. One of the strongest relationships is one that has struggled because the two partners are so different. Their new and healthier focus can involve taking what they've learned and sharing it with other people who are struggling. There are tremendous opportunities in a Helper-Helpee relationship to discover areas where individual growth can take place, resulting in a more mature, loving, and giving relationship for both husband and wife.

Many couples are tempted to maintain the status quo even though they do not like it. Change is an unknown quantity, and there is no guarantee that it will succeed. They need to realize that by equalizing the relationship, they will enjoy each other more. Instead of a "parent-child" relationship, they can treat each other as equal adults. The results will be rewarding.

The Helper-Helpee Marriage

	Behavior	Feelings
Helper	Parenting, counselor	Sensitive, needs to be needed
Helpee	Childish, counselee	Overwhelmed, vulnerable

Theme—Helping/Problems
Major Problem—Dependency
Secondary Problems—Family of Origin and Low Self-Esteem
Major Strength—Empathy/Sensitivity

CHAPTER 7

The Macho Marriage

When I hear the word "macho," my mind is flooded with images of John Wayne, the leather reins of his horse clenched in his teeth, charging single-handedly toward three desperadoes, a rifle in one hand and his Colt 45 blazing in the other.

This image accurately reflects the Macho marriage personality. It's dominated by a husband (in almost every case) who is powerful and competitive and who believes that a real man has to be tough, never showing weakness or sensitivity. In this relationship, his word is law. All is fine as long as the wife cooperates.

Wayne and Wanda have this kind of marriage. She was 19 years old when they met in the singles' group of her church. He was 20, a transfer to the local university, and a new Christian, having asked Christ to be his Savior less than a year before. He actively participated in the discussion and shocked her because he was so opinionated. He insisted that his view was right and would not back down. Wanda was attracted to his undaunted behavior, yet also felt that he was insensitive to other people.

Wayne had noticed Wanda's long brown hair and pretty features earlier in the evening. It happened that their cars were parked next to each other, so he introduced himself. He also noticed that her zippy little sports car was a far cry from his clunker. The next Sunday he teasingly asked if he could drive her car, and promised her a Coke as a reward. They had a great time laughing and telling stories.

After a few months of dating, Wanda's initial uneasiness slipped away except for one area. Usually Wayne was charming and considerate, but sometimes he would compliment her with an accompanying barb such as "You're fun to be with, and by the way I like your car and then you. Ha!" She didn't know if he was serious or just trying to get a rise out of her. Most of the time she took it with a forced smile, hoping the conversation would move on to some other topic.

There were several times when she tried to confront him: "Wayne, that hurts. Please don't say that anymore." Wayne would react, "I didn't mean to hurt you. If that hurt, you must be a big baby. That's ridiculous!" That made her feel put down, and often those dates ended with her in tears.

Wanda's parents liked Wayne and he really liked them. Her family was almost as appealing to him as she was: They were great people, full of warmth, commitment, and understanding. Wayne's childhood home was laced with problems—alcoholism, abuse, siblings in foster homes, truancy, and trouble with the law. Wayne had learned how to survive fights with his dad, siblings, and peers. Even though Wanda's family wasn't perfect, it was far better than his rough heritage.

Wanda was a sensitive girl when they started dating. She wanted to please her parents, friends, and especially Wayne. She hated conflict, and in order to keep peace she would not say anything if she thought it would cause hurt feelings. The parenting she received was well-intended, but Mom and Dad had a habit of finding fault with her shortcomings. She was average in school and took little initiative with anything. This upset Wanda's parents, and in their exasperation they criticized her: "You only got a 'C' in that course?" "If you'd work a little you could do much better." "Are you going to lie around the rest of your life?" "I told you to get the house dusted by 4:30, and now it's 5:00—can't you do what you're told?" The steady diet of put-downs contributed to her skinny self-esteem. At times she would yell back, but usually she stood in a silent stupor, secreting signpost tears.

Wayne's newfound faith made Wanda nervous at times. He would talk to the waitress and gas station attendant, and wanted her to help pass out tracts on the street corner. She had attended church all her life and had become a Christian as a seven-year-old through her mother's direction. Church was okay, but it did not thrill her. Wayne insisted that she become more spiritual, but her personality and inoculated Christian experience curtailed her progress. She wanted to please him, but she could not make herself do some of the things he demanded.

Rather than patiently allowing Wanda to grow at her own pace, Wayne pushed. One day he said, "You must not love me if you don't do the things that are important to me." She tried to explain: "Wayne, you don't understand. I do love you, but I can't do some of this stuff." "Yes, you can," he responded with a glare and slightly flushed cheeks. He stormed off, she felt terrible, and nothing was resolved. After an awkward cooling-off period, they reconnected. Unfortunately, that was typical of how they dealt with conflict—Wayne attacked and Wanda crumbled.

Wayne had clear convictions about how their marriage should work. He wanted to do everything by the book—his book. But a bigger problem was how he enforced compliance. He was abrasive, like sandpaper rubbing against a baby's skin. Wayne coerced, pushed, threatened, accused, and issued ultimatums. It was important for him to be in charge of his marriage and to appear like he was successful.

Wanda was unsure whether Wayne did these things for her or to look good in the eyes of other people. He was picky and demanding: "How come you didn't get the house picked up— do you expect me to live like a slob?" or "Make dinner—I'm hungry!" She felt used: "All I am is a cheap slave that has sex with him on the side." Sometimes it helped for her to remember that he came from a rough background, but she still felt she deserved better treatment.

One day, in the midst of a disagreement, he lifted his fist to hit her. Fortunately, he caught himself. Shocked and dismayed, he walked out of the house. "What's happening to me?" he asked as he wandered the street. He had sworn never to treat his wife like his dad treated his mother. But it was happening anyway. After he apologized, Wanda wanted to draw close to him, yet she was afraid. It was like being next to a ticking time-bomb, not knowing when it is going to explode.

Wayne and Wanda have accumulated many good memories—vocational development, the birth of two children, good friends, and a lay ministry outreach. However, Wayne is frustrated by his wife's inability to deal with issues and she is overwhelmed by his harshness. Wanda is always on guard,

and Wayne vacillates between being demanding and avoiding her when he is upset. Occasionally the situation explodes
with Wayne's angry demands and Wanda's nervous tears.

• • •

   Macho marriages cover a broad range from fairly healthy
to very unhealthy relationships. This is a male-dominated
relationship, with Mrs. Macho standing in the wings as a
combination wife and servant. My experience suggests that
about 12 percent of marriages fit this category. With the shift
in attitudes about men and women and their roles, this marriage personality is not as prevalent today as it once was.
   Some Macho couples are very happy with their relationship
because it meets their need for structure, direction, and
security. Others are devastated because of the ever-escalating
abrasiveness of the relationship. Many ask me if this marriage
can ever change. To be honest, it can change only with effort
and affirmation by both parties. Let's examine the background
and characteristics of this personality, and find some ways to
improve it.

Beginnings

   The source of the Macho marriage can be traced to the
families of origin. The family experience for both partners has
a significant impact on how they view themselves and what
they expect in a marriage relationship. Usually the macho man
comes from a family where relationships were not at a
premium. As an adult, he may not know or care where his
siblings live. He has taken care of himself since age 12 or so.
He has learned that it's a "dog-eat-dog" world and that you're
a fool if you trust anybody.
   Dad and Mom had a poor marriage. He never saw his parents
hug and would be shocked if his dad ever expressed any
affection for him. As a boy, he heard more about what he did
wrong than what he did right. Our macho man learned from
his dad and peers that a "real man" never shows weakness
or talks about his fears. He learned to ignore his feelings and,
worse yet, to deny that he even had feelings of fear, regret,
loneliness, or sadness. His muscles have covered an emotional

vacuum. He is a tough guy who will get the job done, but in the process he rapes relationships.

Mrs. Macho's family experience left her with limited self-confidence. Somehow, she never learned that she was an okay person. She feels bad about herself and guilty for not being better. Either Mom and Dad did not reassure her, or else they were "on her case" all the time. Her feelings were ignored or put down. As a teenager she was shy or hostile, but in either case it was an overreaction to her poor self-view. She left home questioning her worthiness and feeling unloved—and that somehow it was her fault.

When they start dating, his outward, positive, controlling manner provides an immediate sense of security for her. Even though he can be pushy at times, she likes his strength. His muscles or social prowess look so comforting that she doesn't consider the fact that his strength can also be used against her. For example, he may push a physical relationship in dating. If she says no, he may issue an ultimatum: "Either we make out or I'll go with someone else." It's not unusual for her to succumb to his threats and afterward feel sorrow. Yet there are enough rewarding experiences in the premarital relationship to convince her that things will be okay in the marriage.

Outward Style

Occasionally we still see "caveman" jokes in the comics. Typically, the "caveman" appears rough and gruff. He has a club in one hand and with the other is dragging his fair maiden by her hair. Mrs. Caveman looks bewildered and overwhelmed. He is the conqueror and she is the conquered, leaving no doubt about who is in charge.

Some Macho marriages are very much like the caveman relationship: He barks and she jumps. He gives the impression that he owns her. She is both afraid of him and dependent upon him. Her behavior may be submissive, quiet, shy, and nervous, or she can be defiant, argumentative, and challenging. He may not be outwardly gruff, but rather subdued, stern, persistent, and sarcastic. In some cases the Macho marriage is not overtly male oppressive. He may be laid back and somewhat sensitive and she may be outwardly adequate. However, when push comes to shove, he makes sure that he wins what he wants to win. He maintains control and she backs down because he is more forceful physically, verbally, or intellectually.

The macho man comes in many forms—truck driver, construction worker, drill sergeant, sales manager, or corporate hatchet man. He is black-and-white in his thinking and has a reputation that "you don't cross him or he'll get you." He really wants people to like him, but the only method he knows is to literally *make* them. He's afraid that his wife, if given the choice, would reject him, so he keeps her in line. Often he demands, "Get me a cup of coffee!" without any "please" or "thank you."

Mrs. Macho is usually friendly, sensitive, and cooperative. She likes things to go smoothly, so she spends her energy avoiding conflict. This usually means giving in to her husband's wishes. Because she has doubts about her ability to handle life, she tries to please other people so that her immediate environment will feel secure and stable.

This marriage looks like a traditional one, with the man as head of the house and the woman as homemaker and caretaker for the children. The relationship is often interwoven with traditional male/female sex role stereotyping. Men are strong, brave, and rational; women are weak, naive, and emotional. Men bring home the money and women do the housework. She takes the role of being servant, as if she deserved nothing better. While he goes to the races or golfing, or to a pro game with the guys, she stays home with the kids.

It is not uncommon for two Christians in a Macho marriage to misuse the Bible. He uses the Bible as a weapon to prove that he is the head of the house. His wife must be submissive and cooperate with his decisions. Obviously, the intent of Scripture has been misappropriated. The husband uses the Bible to maximize his position while she thinks, "If God is on his side, then He's against me." Sadly, some women think they're disobeying God anytime they do not go along with their husband's wishes.

Their sexual relationship is usually a physical release for him and an ordeal for her. There is little romance or foreplay. He wants sex and it is her job to give it. She seldom reaches a climax, adding to her list of life's disappointments. Where once she felt lovingly conquered, now she feels manhandled.

You might be getting the impression that Macho marriages

are always volatile. Actually some are very pleasant, and the couples involved feel secure in them. However, those who do need help often don't get it because the husband is resistant to counseling. Sometimes the wife will come alone, without her husband knowing it. These marriages can be traumatic, characterized by violence and alcohol abuse. Often she enhances his drinking problem by cooperating rather than confronting. I have encountered situations where she will not have him committed for treatment because he has threatened to leave her, beat her, or "make her pay." She goes along because she doesn't know of any alternatives. As she becomes more burdened and defeated, he becomes angrier.

Man	Woman
Macho (controlling)	Respect (sometimes out of fear)
Upset	Bewildered
Attacking/Mean	Broken

Inward Experience

What is this couple's internal condition? Do these people like themselves? Actually both partners have a low sense of personal worth. Below his gruff exterior there is fear—fear of losing control, or being embarrassed, or having his internal weakness exposed. He focuses on weaknesses in other people in order to avoid facing his own. Noncompliance from others is met with swift reprisal because of his personal insecurity. In addition to Mr. Macho's fear and self-doubt, he may also suffer from low self-esteem, which is expressed in his tendency to be sarcastic, critical, or jealous.

The wife also doubts her worth and thus questions whether she deserves to be treated in a respectable manner. She constantly second-guesses her attempts to please him. Because she is on edge, it is not uncommon for her to repeat "mistakes" for which he has previously reprimanded her. While outwardly submissive, she rehearses her inadequacy or fantasizes about "telling him a thing or two."

What she doesn't realize is that she is very much in control of the marriage. That probably sounds illogical. But she often sets up her husband's undesirable behavior with her struggling self-worth and insecurity. This gives her an excuse not to grow and saves her from the risk of attempting to be a more complete person. She can even "use" her husband to punish her for being inadequate. When she serves supper late and he criticizes her, her "mistake" and his "discipline" reinforce her subconscious belief that she should be punished for worthlessness.

Strengths and Weaknesses

A major strength of the Macho marriage is structure. Because of Mr. Macho's role-orientation and need for control, the marriage and family tend to have a predictable, weekly schedule. Also, everyone knows what is expected regarding rules, household chores, manners, and beliefs. There is a clear line of authority, so most family members feel some security. The parents do as much for their children as possible. Because Dad has high expectations and will not tolerate many mistakes, the children are survivors. They may not have close feelings for Dad, but they do know what it takes to make it in the world.

The Macho marriage usually has two main areas of weakness: lack of warmth and excessive role-orientation. Both are signs of insecurity. By lack of warmth I mean that they are not comfortably loving each another. Because they feel insecure, they are more sensitive to how they are being loved than to how they can love each other. He may think, "She is not very affectionate" instead of, "How can I show her that I really love her?"

I believe this couple is too secretive. They desperately want to be loved but try to get love in unproductive ways. He "asks" for love when he complains about her lack of affection. She "asks" for love when she is nice to him. Neither of them can figure out what is happening. Somehow she is supposed to know that his complaint is really a request: "Will you show me that you love me?" He is supposed to know that a fresh-baked pie is a request: "Will you show me that you care?"

The second area of difficulty is excessive role-orientation. Mr. Macho is embarrassed if anyone in his family does something that, in his mind, does not fit what is appropriate for men, women, boys, and girls. He objects to his daughter

playing Little League baseball. His son must never cry, for that
is a sign of weakness. Such control may work until the children
move into adolescence and peer-group involvement. Then they
are quite capable of sabotaging Dad's control.

Problems occur when Mrs. Macho breaks rules. If Mrs.
Macho goes back to work outside the home, she finds that other
people do not live the way she lives. She may conclude that
she has been mistreated for too long. Unfortunately, she may
overreact when others encourage her not to put up with it
anymore. If she starts throwing ultimatums at her husband,
there will be fireworks, but little progress. She soon learns that
it does not pay dividends to "fight fire with fire."

Fortunately, there are some things that she can do to help
her situation.

Improving the Marriage

Mrs. Macho can influence her husband by responding to him
with confidence, and by calling his bluffs. Suppose her husband
demands, "Get me a cup of coffee." She could respond, "Get
the cup of coffee yourself." However, he will take that as
defiance, and the results won't be pleasant. A better option
is to calmly say, "Honey, I'll be glad to get it for you in a minute, when I get done with my project." Or she could say, "You
know, dear, I don't mind getting your coffee, but it works better
and I'm more cheerful when someone says 'please' to me."

Now the wife is confronting, but with a touch of humor. She
is not attacking, but neither is she retreating. The results are
even better if she says it with a smile. She could even gently
tease him with, "I'm sure you can say 'please.' I know it's in
you. Why don't you try it sometime? You never know what
kind of a good response you might get from me."

Of course, Mr. Macho may not be humored and may respond
with a louder ultimatum: "I said, I want my coffee now!" This
is when she can't back down. Maintaining the same calm,
loving tone of voice, she can say, "I'm sorry if you *must* be
upset, but I'm busy right now, and it will be a few minutes
before I will bring you some coffee."

What she is doing is establishing her own identity without
putting down her mate. In fact, she'll probably feel closer to
him because she is not so afraid. She does not have to wear

a "Tread on me" sweatshirt. She needs to take care of herself and get beyond the belief of "This is all I deserve." She'll discover that she can still cooperate with other people while being her own person.

When Mrs. Macho confronts her husband, it's important that she also reassure him. He might take personal offense if she wants to join a bowling league on her own. She could say something like, "Honey, I really want to join this league so I can spend time with some of my friends. I don't want you to take it personally. I enjoy being with you, but I can be a better wife if I take a break once a week and am involved with this group." Note that as she confronts him she also reassures him that she loves him and that this will ultimately help both of them. It's another way of gently sidestepping his tendency to issue ultimatums.

Some readers may object that this wife is not being submissive. We need to realize that biblical submission does not mean acting like a doormat and allowing the husband to crush the wife emotionally. Submission is taking the responsibility for our spiritual and marital life. If a man is hurting his wife, she does both of them a disservice if she doesn't confront him. She doesn't have to do it in a hostile or demeaning manner. However, she may need some coaching from a caring friend in order to do it in a direct but positive way.

A good biblical example for the wife of a macho man is Moses. He felt powerless and gave God many reasons why he could not do what God told him to do. Moses needed to look beyond his feelings of weakness to God Himself. God promised to supply all of the power Moses needed. In the same way, Mrs. Macho can deal with her need for love and security by being more assertive, direct, and honest, relying on God's strength to go beyond her natural tendency to accept things as they are.

There's also a biblical model for the husband. He is somewhat like the apostle Paul—confident, assertive, and goal-oriented. Paul wanted to maintain his strength and power, but God showed him (in 2 Corinthians 12:7-10) that he needed to learn how to be strong in his weakness. Our macho man needs to discover that he can channel his strength by listening to his wife. Unfortunately, it may take a major disappointment to motivate him to do so. He needs to see how he hurts her;

then maybe he will work on improving his interpersonal skills.

The most important thing a husband can do for this marriage is to support his wife as an individual. Compliments and encouragement will do a lot for her self-image. He might try saying things like "You had a lot of good things to say tonight at the meeting" or "Honey, if you get time, will you call Sears about the special?" or "You know, Dear, if that is something you want to do, there's no doubt in my mind that you can do it. I'm for you 100 percent." The more Mr. Macho honors his wife, the more she will blossom.

It is extremely important that Mr. Macho learn how to make requests of his wife rather than present demands. His normal habit pattern is to tell people what he wants, when he wants it, and how he wants it done. It would help if he prayed and asked God to give him an awareness and sensitivity to his wife's feelings.

Mr. Macho is usually a very proud person, and therefore it is difficult and unappealing to him to appear humble or weak. He must realize that Jesus demonstrated His greatest strength when it appeared He was weak. First Peter 2:23 says, "While being reviled, He did not revile in return; while suffering, He uttered no threats, but kept entrusting Himself to Him who judges righteously." Jesus demonstrated that He was strong enough to leave His case in God's hands, even though He was being treated unfairly. He did not defend Himself because He knew that God would defend Him.

The macho husband can grow in his relationship with Christ by learning through his marriage to submit himself. For example, in the sexual arena, he might concentrate on giving his wife pleasure. By not always having his own way, he demonstrates true strength. That will make an impact on his spouse, for she will feel truly loved and will begin to experience freedom to be who she is. She will become a better wife, and that will benefit him too!

The Macho Marriage

	Behavior	Feelings
Mr. Macho	Challenging, controlling	Inadequate, untrusting
Mrs. Macho	Cautious, unassertive	Undeserving, bewildered

Theme—Dominant, Submissive
Major Problem—Self-Orientation
Secondary Problem—Family of Origin
Major Strength—Structure (Roles defined)

CHAPTER 8

The Pretense Marriage

Hal and Holly met in an unusual way: They happened to be at the same hotel attending different conferences. One morning while having breakfast in the coffee shop, Hal asked for some sugar from Holly's table. Later that day they ran into each other again and exchanged information about their respective conferences. He was attending a meeting for Vietnam veterans. She was representing her university music department at a seminar about teaching music theory to children.

Neither remembers why, but they decided to meet that evening for dinner. There they were, two total strangers, sitting in the restaurant exchanging life stories. Hal had coal-black hair, a mustache and beard, and wire-rimmed glasses. His was a rough background. He had had problems with his stepfather and he hated school. He finally joined the Army to get out on his own. The effects of the war on his fellow vets, both psychologically and physically, concerned him, and he was very vocal about his belief that the military should do more than they were presently doing.

Holly was slightly overweight, dressed in a tan outfit with pleated skirt and matching top. Her hands were empty of rings and her face was accented by little makeup. The second of two girls, she had grown up in a musical family. She had devoted most of her life to music at the expense of her social life. To Holly, Hal's life looked intriguing. And Hal couldn't believe that Holly was so naive.

The remainder of the week became a blur as Hal and Holly spent every available minute together. By the time their conferences were over, they did not want to separate. Holly's parents resisted their attempts to get together, but the more they resisted, the more Holly wanted to see Hal. The attraction she felt for Hal was a mystery to her. She only knew that it was exciting to be with him. Family and friends tried to reason with her, but the warnings only pushed her closer to Hal. Finally she left home, university, and music, and they were married.

Not long after the marriage, Hal and Holly both wished that their chance meeting had never taken place. Holly finally saw what her parents and others had warned her about. Hal was so different that she could not relate to him. Now that she had to live with him, she was no longer intrigued by his differences. What she thought was love had been infatuation. Hal got tired of her being naive and straight. He decided he didn't want to be "reformed" after all. They even had trouble being in the same car because he wanted to listen to country-western or pop rock and she wanted to hear the university station that played classical music.

When it came to truly caring for each other, everything seemed forced. He still had his ways; she still had hers. There was little common ground, and their attempts to work together seemed fruitless. It was not that Hal didn't like Holly, but just that he couldn't relate to her because she was so different. Holly felt sorry for Hal and his hard life experiences, but that was not the same as loving him.

Hal and Holly settled into a roommate relationship. Her activities and interests were in no way similar to his. He worked at the local garage and she found a job with the symphony. He picked up a few friends from the garage; she spent most of her time with other music buffs. They had separate bedrooms, checking accounts, work schedules, and TV sets. Hal would say to himself, "She is a respectable and capable person, but she just doesn't turn me on." Holly thought, "I can't understand what he sees in his rough friends and why he lives the way he does. What was I thinking when I married him?"

Both Hal and Holly feel bad about what has happened, but they can't figure out any significant solutions. Still, they maintain the relationship, not wanting to hurt each other and still hoping that things might change.

Occasionally I run into a Hal and Holly in my office. I

immediately sense that they need a "respirator" to help them maintain marital life. Usually they aren't looking for a marital counselor but a marital *coroner*—someone to pronounce the relationship dead. It is easy for me to end up working harder on their marriage than they do, but I quickly explain that their marital limbo will not change without effort. They have to decide to work at it, and if they do, I'm willing to help.

The Pretense marriage is a "make-believe" relationship. Just as synthetic diamonds look like the real thing, the Pretense marriage is a synthetic imitation. Sure, there is a legal agreement between the two parties, but there is little in the way of a real marriage. They have different interests, backgrounds, goals, and values. They seem unable to connect in love and intimacy. Their relationship is neither passionate nor hostile; at best it's lukewarm. Marital magnetism, infatuation, romance, and enthusiasm are foreign feelings.

Pretense marriages make up only 3 percent of all marriages. In the past more Pretense marriages were consummated because of social and moral patterns. For example, many premarital-pregnancy marriages and arranged relationships were imitation marriages. Also, in the past it was more difficult to be single than it is today, so marriage often happened for survival rather than for commitment. There are fewer arranged and "for-survival" marriages today, and certainly premarital pregnancy no longer automatically prompts marriage. Also, couples are more likely to terminate a Pretense marriage, chalking it up to "bad judgment" or "a mistake."

Beginnings

In most Pretense marriages there is more outward pressure for the couple to marry than inward desire. There are several situations that seem to feed Pretense marriages, such as when one or both partners are rebounding from a bad relationship. Occasionally a Pretense marriage is arranged by family and friends. The family believes it is a perfect match, and the children are obedient, hoping that it will work out. Wealthy families have been known to do the picking for their sons and daughters. During the Vietnam War some marriages took place to avoid the draft. Occasionally a widower marries only because he needs a "mother" for his children. Unmarried pastors looking for a church have married because they believed they would improve their chances for a pastoral position. All in all, when I see a Pretense marriage relationship I usually find external pressure for the marriage rather than any strong romantic striving for each other.

Outward Style

This couple is usually friendly and cordial. They are not out to "get" the other party, nor are they attracted to the other party. They seem like good friends rather than lovers. In contrast, most married people act like they are connected to one another by showing affection or even conflict. But the pretense couple does not deeply experience love or hate in the hurts or joys of each other because they are not emotionally connected.

Their physical relationship is more mechanical than romantic. Sex takes place on rare occasions, and one or both may fantasize about other partners during their sexual encounter. They tend to be silent not only in public but also at home. He may have a favorite chair in the family room, she a special hobby to keep her busy. Sitting at the dinner table is like being a guest at a friend's home rather than being with your family. Both tend to get involved in third-party activities such as their children's hobbies, pets, jobs, and friends. They are very much like married singles—to the extreme. Unfortunately, affairs are not unusual among one or both partners.

Socially, this couple shows no red flags. Actually you don't see them together much socially because they travel in separate circles. Sometimes this is a marriage where both partners are more interested in their professions, and marriage is a secondary concern, held onto for conscience sake but not holding a high priority in their lives.

Inward Experience

For individuals in the Pretense marriage, the biggest challenge is dealing with their lack of feelings. Their inner struggle is "How do I force myself to care for someone to whom I do not feel attracted?" This is by and large a secret that neither discusses with the other, for they realize that such a discussion would not be productive.

In addition, this couple has never fully committed themselves to the relationship. And because the numbness and sense of entrapment is so overpowering, they begin to live for other purposes than the marriage. There is a sense of hopelessness that there is no reasonable solution to their dilemma.

Strengths and Weaknesses

There is some strength to the Pretense marriage, and it revolves around structure. Even though there is little emotional exchange between Mr. and Mrs. Pretense, they do maintain a structure for themselves and their children. This provides security for the children and a sense of order to the family. It is difficult to suggest any other strengths in the relationship because the very essence of the Pretense marriage is the lack of relationship.

Absense of emotional attraction is the primary weakness of the Pretense marriage. Certainly, marriage is not exclusively dependent upon romance, but in this case the lack of emotional attachment and romantic feeling undercuts their ability to have a "real" rather than a synthetic marriage.

Improving the Marriage

The Old Testament describes marriage as a process of leaving, cleaving, and becoming one flesh. We are told in Genesis 2:24 that God's plan is, "A man shall leave his father and his mother, and shall cleave to his wife; and they shall become one flesh." In this particular marriage relationship, the couple has left their parents but have trouble cleaving or bonding to each other to become one flesh (emotional and physical attraction).

The solution is not so much whether or not they should divorce, but whether they want to get married. Though this couple is legally married, they need to become emotionally married. I realize that it is impossible to force someone to love another person, but it is possible to *learn* to love another person. That may be a limited possibility, but it is better than living emotionally separated lives.

This couple is in a position where they need to seek Christ to provide the power and energy to love each other beyond their own capabilities. They must realize that they can't manufacture love without help from the Lord. The very fact that they are in need of a deeper level of love for their spouse makes them eligible to receive from God as only He can provide.

I must also present a caution: Take it slow and easy. It is important to keep regular contact, but it is also important not to expect an immediate rejuvenation of strong positive feelings. I also recommend that the couple in the Pretense marriage make themselves available to a trained marriage counselor. If either individual begins to feel guilty or angry because he is not attracted to his spouse, that will only serve to further separate them. Possibly through counseling, the individual can admit to the lack of feelings in a healthier way, opening the door for the growth of warm feelings.

Finally, energy needs to be spent getting into the relationship, not out of it. It will take commitment, but some couples in this position have discovered that concerted effort by both sides has resulted in enlivened and enriched relationships. It takes work and desire, but it can be accomplished.

The Pretense Marriage

	Behavior	Feelings
Husband	Individual activity	Numb, lonely
Wife	Individual activity	Numb, lonely

Theme—Lack of Romantic Attraction
Major Problem—Commitment
Major Strength—Structure

CHAPTER 9

The Kids' Marriage

This chapter is about premature marriages. The Kids' marriage is a union between two children who are not ready to face the difficulties of life on their own. Like a premature child who needs neonatal intensive care, this couple needs "intensive care" until they grow up. Their lives are filled with one marital crisis after another. The following event is typical of a Kids' marriage.

Jake's boss told him he had earned a raise of 30 cents an hour. His job at the car dealership as the cleanup man was paying off. He and his wife, Jackie, could sure use the extra money, too. When he arrived home, he proudly announced his good news to Jackie and said he was going out to celebrate with his friend, Sonny. "Just the two of you?" she asked. "Yeah, we're going to the Airliners' game!" he said, not thinking that his wife might want to go too. Jackie didn't mind Jake spending time with Sonny, but she did not trust Sonny's girlfriend, Ann.

Jackie waited up for Jake, but he didn't show. Taking matters into her own hands, she went looking for him at a favorite restaurant. He was there, all right, and so was Sonny, Ann, and another girl. The four of them looked like they were having a great time. Jackie fumed all the way home: "That dirty, rotten creep. If he thinks he can get away with this, he'd better think again."

An hour later, Sonny let Jake off and went on home. Jake tried to open the door, but it was locked. He tried his key and turned the knob, but something was barricaded against the door. "What's going on here?" he yelled.

Then he heard Jackie yelling at him. "Going out with Sonny

alone, huh? I saw you, all four of you, up at the restaurant. You creep, I'll never trust you again! Your clothes are outside in the corner.''

Without thinking, Jake started ramming his body into the door. It made him mad that he was accused without even a question. Nobody was going to keep him out of his own apartment! Meanwhile Jackie called her parents and the police.

The door was broken by the time the police arrived, and Jake and Jackie were yelling at the top of their lungs and throwing things at each other. The police tried to settle things down until her parents arrived. Jackie went home with them while Jake took his clothes back inside and sacked out on the couch to guard the entrance to the apartment.

For the next few days, Jake and Jackie were like two siblings in their respective corners, pointing fingers at each other and shouting, "He did it!" Gradually, however, their blame turned to remorse and a little curiosity. "I wonder what she's doing," Jake thought. Jackie wondered, "Maybe I did assume something about Jake and the others at the restaurant."

Jake called Jackie's mom to see how she was. Jackie called Sonny to see how Jake was doing. After a few more days, when things had calmed down, they made up and that night they made love like never before. They were back together as if nothing had ever happened.

Jackie's parents took a deep breath, crossed their fingers, and fervently prayed. They knew that Jake and Jackie could easily go through another "hot war" with just the slightest spark. They didn't know whether to stay out of it or try to help. One thing was certain: Jake and Jackie's feelings for each other changed like the wind. One minute they were madly in love, the next minute they couldn't stand each other.

● ● ●

The Kids' marriage is a little like my early driving experience. I was a 16-year-old kid who thought he knew what he was doing. I considered myself as good as any adult driver until a few minor fender-benders proved me wrong. The Kids' marriage is made up of partially trained "drivers" who experience numerous marital "fender-benders."

Beginnings

They meet in high school, "fall in love," and have a great time together. Their love is actually "puppy love" or infatuation and is rarely more than skin deep. Their relationship develops because both of them have a base of security without the responsibility of providing for themselves. When they have a spat they can go home and cool off, so a relationship problem is not overwhelming.

What they have feels good, but it is also unrealistic. It is one thing to pull off a relationship when all your basic needs are taken care of by your parents; it's quite another to fashion a relationship when you're also responsible for a job, apartment, and daily chores. Once they marry, this couple can't go home and cool off after a spat. Now they must confront each other in difficult circumstances, whereas before they dealt with each other only when it was convenient.

People in Kids' marriages are almost always teenagers. Most of us still have a significant need for development between the ages of 16 and 20. We are still getting our act together with regard to values, goals, spiritual convictions, and vocation. People who marry during this time hinder their personal development. They move into marriage before being successfully weaned from their family of origin.

It is my belief that if each partner in these marriages had continued personal development without marrying, most of them would have chosen a different partner at age 22 than at age 18. If they did choose the same person later on, at least both of them would be better equipped to negotiate the multiple demands of marriage.

Only about 5 percent of all marriages fit the Kids' personality type. And after they have been married two to five years they usually move into one of the other marriage personalities. It is very unusual to find a Kids' marriage in couples that have been married longer than 12 years. They either grow up in their marriage or give up on it.

Outward Style

This marriage is as unpredictable as a typical American teenager. It's energetic, impulsive, independent yet dependent, fun-loving, broke, and absentminded. If it were not so serious at times, it could almost be comical. Years later they will laugh about it, but not now. They fight over who should dry the dishes and clean the bathroom. He becomes jealous when she tells him about some guy who made a pass at her at work, and he might give her a spanking for being "bad." They tend to spend as much time with their single friends as with each other.

The Kids' marriage is usually very active. It is normal for these two people to fight, then make up, then fight again, then make up, and so on. Usually their parents are very much involved, trying to bail the kids out of financial disaster or help them find an apartment. It's not uncommon for other people to become involved as well, such as the court system, a social worker, a family abuse center, or the neighborhood church trying to help with food or clothing. This couple rarely operates on their own because of their childish, immature behavior.

Inward Experience

What this couple think and feel inside is related to how they behave. When they are outwardly impulsive they are also thinking and feeling impulsively. When something happens to them, they don't think about the impact of their reactions. They just react! For example, if Jake's friend Sonny gets a new stereo and Jake decides he wants one too, he buys it. So what if the rent is due next week and they need grocery money? It is an impulsive act, based upon current emotions, without thought for the future.

Their emotions are felt to the fullest. When they are angry they are really angry, and when they are jealous they are really jealous, and when they are loving they are really loving. They can be intimidated by mature adults. It is difficult for these kids to admit that they have needs or to take advice from others. They experience an unsettling fear that they are not as "together" as others, but behave defiantly when confronted with their inadequacies. For example, if a parent confronts Jake about using rent money to buy the stereo, Jake's response may be "Look, Mom, if you're going to give me a lecture, forget it. I'll get the rent money somewhere else."

Strengths and Weaknesses

The major strength and weakness of this marriage relationship is the same—its youth. Because they are young and energetic, this couple can adjust to difficult and trying circumstances and forget bad experiences without falling prey to bitterness. After they fight and make up they move on instead of being resentful.

But youth is also a weakness. These two people are immature and not ready to carry on the responsibilities of a marriage. That is not to say they do not love and care for each other, for frequently they do. However, they enter into this tremendous responsibility ill-equipped to fulfill the task of relating to and being responsible for each other.

Another weakness is their high degree of self-focus. They are not objective, and frequently they are overly sensitive and reactive. It is difficult for them to see life from someone else's perspective. When two people are focused upon themselves, the task of working together as a team becomes far more challenging.

Hopefully a Kids' marriage has another source of strength: Most young couples can benefit from the wisdom of their parents or other concerned adults. A Kids' relationship is like a canoe tossed about on the ocean. Parents, like a large ship, can come alongside to protect the canoe. This gives a couple time to mature until they can handle the "ocean" on their own. Advice on housing, finances, jobs, and education (and at times even financial assistance) can make the difference in this couple surviving their premature marriage.

Improving the Marriage

Not only does this couple need contact with their parents and other interested couples, but they need to be in a situation where they have to answer to someone. This is best accomplished by answering to a couple or a pastor who is not family-related. They should meet with this mature couple at least once a month to review their marital, financial, spiritual, and vocational lives. This will give them a chance for regular feedback and will provide a systematic approach toward reaching maturity.

When I have a couple like this in counseling, I am very direct and confrontive. Because they act like children, I treat them like children. I do not ask them to do an assignment—I tell them. I do not ask them to be nice to each other—I tell them. But it is important to verbalize confidence at the same time you are guiding them. I tell them that they will grow up and start acting more mature one of these days. However, until they do, they are going to have to put up with other people guiding their lives.

Another thing they should do is attend a couple's seminar or retreat at least once every six months. This will give them helpful training as well as contact with other young couples. It also helps if they get involved in some type of couples' Bible study or fellowship group where they can have regular, ongoing interaction with other couples.

When they get into problems, it is extremely important that they not try to resolve these problems alone. Their immaturity will probably sabotage most of their well-intentioned efforts. They need some objective, outside advice and help in order to maintain marital stability.

I am not suggesting that you do everything for a Kids' couple or shield them from the consequences of their impulsive, immature behavior. If she wants a divorce because they had a fight and he spanked her, then sit down with her. Let her talk about her feelings, but help her see that a divorce is overreacting to the fight.

Studies have concluded that as many as nine out of ten teenage marriages end in divorce, most within the first two years of marriage. The most important thing we can tell a teenage couple is to wait it out. If they can follow the direction of mature family and friends, and survive the tough growing-up years, there is definitely hope for this marriage.

The Kids' Marriage

	Behavior	Feelings
Husband	Impulsive, boastful,	Questioning, oppositional
	Mistake-prone	Mood swings
Wife	Impulsive, mistake-prone	Unsure, afraid, mood swings

Theme—Immaturity
Major Problem—Self-Orientation
Secondary Problem—Family of Origin
Major Strength—Energy of Youth

CHAPTER 10

The Active-Active Marriage

So far we've examined six marriage personalities. Though all six have their relative strengths, we have observed that, left unattended, each personality has built-in weaknesses that can destroy the marriage. This last personality fits about 20 percent of all marriages, and tends to be the most stable.

The Active-Active marriage personality is one in which both partners have individually decided to "put their best foot forward" in the relationship. They also are well-equipped with the abilities and talent to pull off a good marriage. Just what do we mean by "well-equipped"? A well-prepared marriage partner is one who is mature and directed, has resolved the past, has a good family model, is content with self, is giving and approachable, and values God, other people, and himself. If this sounds like a "Super Spouse," that is not my intention. It is simply a fact that some people are better equipped to succeed in marriage.

An example from a fifth-grade teaching situation illustrates my point. The teacher may tell one set of parents, "Your son tries hard and does as well as he can, given his capabilities. But he is not an 'A' student." To another couple the teacher may say, "Your son has a great deal of potential, but he is not working; he's only doing the minimum." Note that one student has the potential, but is not committed, while the other student has the commitment, but not as much potential. An Active-Active marriage is made up of people who have the potential for an excellent relationship *and* the commitment to make it happen. Let's look at one such marriage.

Jerry was 24 and Barb 22 when they met through a mutual friend in a large Southern city. Jerry was a successful computer programmer, thanks to the training and experience he received while in the Navy. She was preparing to graduate from college.

While Jerry appeared settled, his youth had been turbulent. Much of his life he had acted like a bowling ball, deliberately knocking over everything that got in his way. As a teenager he rebelled against his parents' discipline and spiritual leadership. Consequently he tried just about everything which could lead to trouble. Eventually he was arrested. The choice was simple: Join the military or go to jail. He chose the military, and while there his drill sergeant, new friends, and being away from home made him examine his life. Soon he stopped fighting his parents, society, and God, and started living responsibly. Now the rebellious years were past, and the valuable lessons learned, plus his programming expertise, personal drive, and individual character, gave him promise of a bright future.

Barb was the second of three girls and had always been reasonably responsible, compliant, and active. Her parents were easygoing, responsible people. Her dad worked at a local factory and her mom had a part-time job to help her daughters through college. Because half the school expenses were hers, Barb also worked part-time, yet she still had time for several extracurricular activities.

Things seemed to "connect" for Jerry and Barb. They had some mutual friends, similar values, and spiritual sensitivity. Jerry was impressed by her aerobic conditioning, her hard work in school, and her spunk. Barb was amazed that Jerry could be aggressive yet also approachable and sensitive to her as a person. They were soon making plans for a big wedding.

It was evident early in the marriage that Jerry and Barb cared deeply for each another and were highly committed to their relationship. Still, their different backgrounds meant considerable adjustment. Jerry's family was strong-willed, assertive, aggressive, and directed. Barb's family was relaxed, easygoing, and fairly nonconfrontive. Different bedtimes, eating habits, forms of entertainment, and conflict-resolving styles produced many challenges for Jerry and Barb to work through.

Barb worked for several years to build up a cash reserve before they had children. Jerry's job continued to improve as his reputation spread in the computer industry. After nearly nine years of marriage, they had two children, ages three and one-and-a-half. They were established in their church and the community and had many friends. But Barb, because she was busy changing diapers and communicating in "toddler language," had lost some of her confidence. She loved the kids, yet they were draining on her. She struggled to remain mentally alert now that she no longer had her job.

One evening when Jerry came home he announced with great excitement that they were moving to the West Coast. Barb tried to go through the motions of affirming and complimenting Jerry on his great challenge and opportunity. She wanted to be excited too, but he had caught her off-guard. In the past they had always talked through major decisions together. She was hurt that instead of talking through this decision, he had simply announced it. Barb was also overwhelmed by the thought of a move.

Later that evening Barb told Jerry that, although she was excited, she was also hurt and wasn't sure if she could handle a move. Jerry was hurt by her words. "Barb, you're not backing me. I'm very disappointed in your lack of support for me, especially when this is such a great opportunity."

"Jerry, I love you," Barb responded, "but I don't think you understand how disoriented I feel. You're asking me to leave close contact with my family, my friends, and my church to move to the West Coast where I know practically no one."

For the next few days, silence reigned in their relationship. Finally, one night after the kids were in bed, they broke through and started talking. Jerry admitted that he was hurt, and that he also knew he had hurt her. "Honey, I'm sorry. I want you to know that even though I really want to take this job, I'm willing not to. The bottom line is that you're more important to me than any job."

Barb broke down and cried when she realized again how much Jerry loved her. They embraced as Barb told Jerry that she was not opposed to moving. "I feel low on energy and confidence. I want to make sure that I can hold up my part of the relationship when we move." As they resolved their conflict and hurt, they talked the rest of the evening about their options. That opened up a whole new arena of creativity as they critiqued the jobs, their future, their goals, and their current situation. Finally they agreed on the decision to move.

Jerry and Barb turned a potentially bad situation into something that was not only better for them individually, but also for their marriage. Throughout their marriage relationship, Jerry and Barb have worked to maintain a balance between their individual endeavors and their joint acitivities. For a few years they jogged together. Later they started playing tennis with friends. That was not only fun for both of them but allowed interaction with other people.

Most of the time Jerry and Barb function well in their marriage. Both choose not to let difficulties and disagreements go unattended. Occasionally they do hurt each other, but soon after the hurt comes forgiveness, resolution, and a continuing, forthright, loving commitment to each other.

Notice in this story how much Jerry and Barb work at having a successful relationship. Many people think a strong commitment only means that there will never be a divorce. There are many nondivorced couples who stay together because of their commitment to marriage, but they are not necessarily fulfilled in their marriage. The Active-Active couple venture beyond that level. They have decided not just to survive their marriage, but to develop and fashion it for individual, mutual, and societal good. Let's look at the elements that make up this personality, and also at ways to understand, maintain, and improve the relationship.

Beginnings

This couple starts their relationship from a position of strength. Often they're in their early or midtwenties when they marry. Because they are older, they've usually finished their education, are established vocationally, and have developed their beliefs and values based upon their own persuasions, not just the persuasions of their parents or society.

Several studies have shown that age 24 for men and 23 for women is the best time to marry. Before that they are like a loaf of half-baked bread: It looks done—browned—on the outside, but it's only thickened batter on the inside. Between the ages of 18 and 22, most individuals need to take a hard look at themselves apart from their family. That's when they can clearly define their own individuality, strengths, abilities, and spiritual drive, and can deal with past hurts they may have experienced. When people have successfully laid the past to rest, accepting the good as well as the bad, they are much more eligible for moving into a positive marriage relationship.

In addition, there are practical reasons for being apart from the family before marriage. People learn to take responsibility for cleaning their laundry, cooking their meals, balancing their checkbooks, and using their time wisely. There is no one else to blame for bad decisions. Between 18 and 22, most of us figure ourselves out and get a healthy start on life, making for significantly less pressure on a marriage.

Outward Style

The general theme of the Active-Active marriage is "intentional commitment." Each partner is a distinct individual with gifts and talents. Each takes responsibility for his own behavior. And each has chosen to be forever attached to the other, working to make their marriage better year after year. This commitment does not come from a feeling of obligation but from a sense of preferring one another.

This couple is not intimidated by difficulties and disaster but takes advantage of them. They are mature enough to recognize the need for cooperation, sacrificing to make the relationship workable and fulfilling. Their relationship is described in Ecclesiastes 4:9-11: "Two are better than one because they have a good return for their labor. For if either of them falls, the one will lift up his companion. But woe to the one who falls when there is not another to lift him up. Furthermore, if two lie down together they keep warm, but how can one be warm alone?"

As I have interviewed Active-Active couples, I have concluded that they truly enjoy each other when they are alone and when they are with other people. Their strength lies in each contributing to the marriage rather than in depending on the marriage. They are givers, not takers; and in giving, each receives.

They attempt to solve their problems quickly. Though they know what they want, there is greater desire to consider what is best for the other person and to accommodate accordingly. Once a problem is solved, it becomes another confirmation of the strength of their marriage relationship, and serves to encourage them in subsequent conflict.

Every marriage has times when one or both partners struggle

with life issues. The Active-Active couple has the knack for supporting each other when there is need. If they are both employed, they take turns encouraging each other's vocational endeavors. They approach parenting as a team. They collaborate on their financial planning, home repair, and vacations.

Mutual support includes listening, objective feedback, and constructive criticism. For example, if the husband is thinking about starting a new business, the wife might say, "I have no doubt you can do it, Honey. But how does this fit in with our other business? And have you considered the number of hours it will take to get it off the ground and keep it going?" Constructive criticism is usually well-received because it comes from someone who believes in him. This same person who confronts him also takes pleasure in his successes. Jealousy is rare. They are even willing to allow each other time off from the relationship for individual growth. This might mean attending a conference for professional purposes or spiritual growth, or just a brief vacation from the "family battle."

Sex is not an ordeal but a good deal. It is truly enjoyed by both partners. Each takes initiative, and there is a fair degree of sexual experimentation. In the midst of foreplay, they inform as well as consult with each other on what is pleasing. Consequently, their sexual encounters are enjoyed and often orgasmic. They have "fun" in the bedroom.

In social situations, this couple is comfortable together. When people visit with them, it is pleasant because this marriage is made up of two people who treat each other with respect. They do not tear each other down with sarcasm but humor and tease each other in a fun-loving and caring way. They believe in each other and they aren't ashamed to hold hands and praise each other publicly. Ironically, even with all this openness, they do not stop being individuals. They are like a figure-skating duo displaying separate moves that are beautifully choreographed into a unified performance.

The predominant feature of an Active-Active marriage is the value this couple places on their relationship. Almost without exception, both partners consider success in marriage more important than any job or social activity. If a job change would weaken the family, they turn down the job offer, despite the potential professional and financial rewards. This doesn't mean that the couple won't get sidetracked at times, but their sensitivity to the marriage relationship usually guides them back to focus on what's best for the marriage.

Time is a pressure point for this couple. If they aren't careful, they can give away all their time to children, jobs, friends, church, hobbies, and shopping and not have any time left for each other. Lack of attention to each other can leave their marriage shipwrecked on the rocky shores of less important things. This doesn't mean that a person who highly values his marriage must have an insignificant job and stay home all the time checking off his "honey-do" list. What I am saying is that the Active-Active couple needs to remember what is most important in life. They must remain disciplined enough to maintain the marriage as the priority. It's not that other activities are eliminated—though some may need to be—but that they are put in their proper place.

Inward Experience

This husband and wife are free to be themselves. Their minds are not crowded with thoughts of protecting themselves from their partner. Confessing their hurts, dreams, frailties, vulnerabilities, and daily successes keeps the relationship fresh and alive.

They rarely, if ever, feel like the other is "out to get them." In fact, they usually feel that the other person is looking out for them. They are also confident that their spouse will be honest with them even when it means a disagreement. This builds tremendous trust. Inwardly, they not only expect loyalty from each other, they also rest in it.

The Active-Active personality has a marathon flavor to it. I am amazed at the stamina of marathon runners. Twenty-six miles of steady plodding is a world apart from a 100-yard dash. Long-distance runners know that they are in for the long haul, not the short puff, and that the best way to finish is to keep a steady pace through the predictable, critical phases of the race. Active-Active couples persevere through the tough stages of adult life. When she has a bad day and feels like her husband is not in tune with her, she does not fall apart. She knows that marital life has its problems, and that things will be better soon because the overall relationship is sound. She has enough common sense to realize that no mate she might have chosen could perform to all expectations or needs all the time.

This couple is objective about married life, allowing for mistakes without becoming pessimistic about the relationship. They may be disheartened, but they soon realize that a mistake is only a temporary setback in the marriage marathon.

Strengths and Weaknesses

The Active-Active marriage personality has many more strengths than weaknesses. One of the major strengths is the maturity level of the partners. They demonstrate maturity by being reponsible to the relationship and by their willingness to attend to their spouse's needs with the same energy that they give to their own needs. Mature people realize that life doesn't always go their way, so they bend and work as team players.

Along with their maturity, they display ability to negotiate. They work through problems rather than around them. When they discuss an issue, both of them are clear about the next step and what to expect from each other.

No doubt another strength is their commitment to the relationship. Their primary focus is on their marriage, and they do not allow other people or situations to infringe on that focus. In addition, they are secure in their respect for each other. They believe in their spouse, hope for his or her best, and genuinely love their partner.

Interpersonal affection is another strength. Children profit from this aspect of the marriage. Mom and Dad love each other and are proud to say it and show it. Hugs, love pats, and kisses are a regular part of this marriage. Children may be embarrassed or amazed at how Mom and Dad continue to find each other interesting.

Because Mom and Dad focus on their relationship, children not only see an example, but at times may feel excluded from their parents. "Marriage first, children second" is this family's motto. This is not to say that the children are not loved: They are. But marital love and affection serve as a primary foundation for parental love and guidance of the children.

There are a few weaknesses in this marriage, and one of them is the distinct identity of the individuals. Sometimes two strong individuals experience conflict because their individual needs seem contradictory. But outsiders are usually more uncomfortable with their intensive conflict than are the couple themselves, who know how to deal with it.

Another weakness is that of exclusiveness. Because these two folks get along so well, they may not feel a need to be involved with many other couples. Their relationship can develop into an "island syndrome," in which they operate independently of others around them. Though this is comfortable for the couple, it is not necessarily healthy in the long run. They can learn from others and also be an example of a productive relationship.

One important area to watch for in the Active-Active marriage is the influence of major life events. Rarely do problems develop from within their relationship. However, external events, such as the birth of children, job changes, layoffs, responsibilities with extended family, or individual traumas, can cause marital struggles. There is never a doubt that they care for each other, but at times they can find themselves being irritable with each other because of outside pressures.

Improving the Marriage

The Active-Active Marriage is not a perfect marriage. Like any other relationship, it is vulnerable to the continued stress and strain of life. This couple needs to rely not only on themselves but also on God. Their greatest danger is in taking the relationship for granted. That is why they need to focus daily on their relationship with Christ. This gives them a solid base from which to reach out to other people. Because they have so much to give, this couple needs to give to others. They also need to continue to monitor their progress and further develop their skills so that they always grow in their relationship.

The Active-Active Marriage

	Behavior	Feelings
Active	Inform, respect, and support individuality	Empathetic, self-accepting

Active   Inform, respect,   Empathetic,
                  and support indi-   self-accepting
                  viduality

Theme—Intentional Commitment
Major Problem—Family of Origin
Secondary Problem—Life Stages
Major Strength—Mutual Collaboration

CHAPTER 11

Common Marital Detours

Of the hundreds of people who have come to me for marital therapy, I have never found one who wanted to create an unhappy marriage. Though most couples start their marriage with high expectations and the best of intentions, some get caught in difficult situations and don't know what to do. Sometimes I say they're victims of marital detours.

When driving a car, it is not uncommon to run into a detour, especially in the summertime. I don't like them, but they are a fact of life. But detours actually serve a useful function: Because of road construction, they provide an alternate route. We don't go looking for detours, but if we ignore them, we find it much harder to reach our destination.

Detours serve a similar function in marriage. We may not like them, but they are real. We can complain, feel bad, feel guilty, and blame our spouse, or we can adjust to the detour and continue along the marriage journey. The secret to healthy married life is not removing the detours, but adjusting to them.

One or two detours should not ruin a marriage. However, when those problems are not resolved, additional detours can be crippling. We have examined the characteristics of healthy marriages, and marriage personalities with their strengths and weaknesses. With that as a foundation, let's look at the most common marital detours. I have classified them into three main areas:

Category One: Relationship Issues

    1) Communication breakdown
    2) Sexual dissatisfaction

3) Loss of hope for a good relationship
4) Values conflict
5) Vacuum of spiritual exchange

Category Two: Personal Issues

1) Negative emotions
2) Numbness—no feelings
3) Victimized
4) Fantasizing

Category Three: External Factors

1) Excessive involvement of friends
or family in the marriage
2) Murphy's Law syndrome
3) Financial stress

Let me clarify that we are not necessarily discussing unstable marriage relationships here. If a couple decides not to divorce because of their Christian beliefs, those beliefs provide protection (stability) around their marriage. Unfortunately, the internal workings of that relationship may be seriously hurting.

When a couple has an unstable marriage, I do not suggest that they escape. Rather, they need to take the initiative toward improvement. Either partner can get the ball rolling by saying something like this: "Look, you're bothered by this relationship, and I am too. What can we do to get out of this rut?" The following issues are potential areas of improvement.

Relationship Issues

1. *Communication breakdown.* One of the most obvious detours to a healthy marriage is dysfunctional communication. This can be reflected in hot wars (shouting) or cold wars (silent grumbling). But this is not just a reflection of the tone of voice; even when there is conversation, many couples cannot resolve their past or present conflicts.

The most common cause of communication breakdown is that individuals dig in their heels and insist on their rights rather than trying to negotiate and compromise. We see this in most marriage personalities. For example, in the

Active-Resistant marriage, the partners go their independent ways. In a Macho marriage, the husband is more interested in winning and exhibiting his power and influence than in doing what is best for the relationship. Hot wars are common in Active-Resistant, Macho, and Kids' personalities; cold wars are more prevalent in Active-Passive, Helper-Helpee, and Pretense relationships.

Because of consistent frustration, silence sometimes becomes the pattern of the communication in a relationship. One or both partners may say very little in order to avoid overt conflict but be hiding frustration and hostility. Other examples of dysfunctional communication in marriage are:

a) Negative behavior—tone of voice which is biting and sarcastic, or negative facial expressions such as sneering, boredom, disgust, or anger.

b) Blaming—consistent attacking in which one or both partners are reminded of their failure and inadequacies.

c) Cross-complaining—a situation in which one partner brings up a topic to discuss, then the other partner adds another topic before the first one is worked through.

d) Multiple focus—an inability to focus on one problem at a time because of the multiple issues that face them.

e) "You" statements—one or both parties use "you" statements such as "You always..." or "You never..." rather than "I" statements, like "I am responsible for..." or "It was my idea and I would like to..."

f) Caustic comments—sarcasm, cynicism, or hitting below the belt. This includes making fun of personal frailties, vulnerabilities, and past hurts.

g) Dredging up the past—bringing up past problems and failures in the midst of conflict as weapons to attack the other person and reinforce one's own position.

Even the best of marriages are not immune from these dysfunctional communication patterns. However, they become a serious problem when a couple consistently uses these methods.

I should point out that communication difficulty may reflect a lack of skill. Some couples want to communicate but struggle at it because they simply do not know how. I've heard many people say, "We just can't communicate." Whenever I hear that, my immediate response is, "That is absolutely not true. You cannot *not* communicate." Everything we do in a marriage relationship is communicating something to our spouse. What they really mean is that they do not like the communication that goes on between them.

There is help available for those who desire to improve their communication skills. They might consult a counselor, or participate in a small group, or read some of the excellent books that are helpful to couples and individuals. Some of these are listed at the back of this book. I have also given additional pointers on effective communication in the chapter titled "Negotiation Skills."

2. *Sexual dissatisfaction.* The frequency and/or quality of sex can often be a frustration. I realize I take a risk in suggesting any normal frequency of sexual intercourse. From my own counseling practice, couples have spanned the range from seven times a day to total abstinence (or one or two times per year). However, one to three sexual encounters per week, or four to twelve times per month, is the usual range.

This is not to suggest that if you do not have sex within that range you are abnormal and wrong, since frequency may be influenced by factors such as the amount of stress related to parenting young children, job responsibilities, physical drive, or how well two people are getting along. Most couples report that frequency varies at different stages in their marital life. Frequency does not necessarily decrease with age. Many couples become sexually rejuvenated when their children are older and they have more time for each other.

Generally, men tend to complain about the lack of frequency in their sexual encounters while women tend to complain about the quality of the sexual encounter. This doesn't necessarily mean that she must have an orgasm every time. Some men measure satisfaction by their wife's orgasm: If she is not orgasmic, they feel emasculated. But women are generally more concerned about whether there was expression of love, caring, tenderness, and responsiveness.

Unhealthy marriages exhibit reduced frequency of physical contact and a lack of compassion in the midst of sexual contact. It is not unusual for a woman in an unhealthy Active-Resistant or Macho marriage to lie in bed at night praying to herself, "Please don't touch me. I can't stand it, and I don't know what I'll do if you try." She lies there in fear that he will want to engage in sexual intercourse when she can't even bear the tension of him being in the same bed. At times she may even feel prostituted in the midst of her own marriage, and may reject any of her husband's advances. On the other hand, a husband can also be the rejecter, denying his wife's sexual desires. Occasionally bitterness is so intense that there is no sexual contact whatever.

3. *Loss of hope.* Some marriages are characterized by loss of confidence and hope. The partners don't know where they are going and have no confidence that things will ever improve. We see this especially in Active-Resistant, Helper-Helpee, and Pretense marriages when long-standing problems are never resolved and a status quo relationship develops. The couple is treading water in the "ocean of marriage." Such a situation often spawns feelings of numbness, bitterness, or depression.

4. *Values conflict.* A serious marital detour is an extreme difference in values. Couples with conflicting ideas in too many areas (such as recreation, hobbies, political parties, food preferences, and spiritual beliefs) will usually experience disharmony. No matter where this couple turns, they find disagreement. It's not that they are intentionally looking to disagree—it's just that they have little in common. They deal with each other only about their disagreements, which seriously upsets marital harmony and balance.

5. *Vacuum of spiritual exchange.* Common spiritual values can cement a marriage. It is hard to destroy a relationship that is built by two people who love God and are committed to obeying His command to love each other. This couple can pray together and for each other. They can confess their needs and exchange ideas, thoughts, or feelings regarding their own personal spiritual walks. When one or both partners don't have such spiritual resources, there is less reserve to deal with the challenges which marriage presents.

This and the other detours we've examined are problems that a couple have in relating to each other. There are also problems that one partner can face that will adversely affect a marriage.

Personal Issues

1. *Negative emotions.* Individuals who are caught in an unhappy marriage frequently experience several negative emotions regarding their relationship. Their "laundry list" includes bitterness, anger, resentment, and fear. These emotions are usually the result of unresolved hurt in the relationship. After years of daily depositing negative feelings, people become so hardened that attempts at melting the negative emotions are like taking on an iceberg with a match.

Marriages where one or both partners have chronic bouts with depression, anxiety, and other personality disturbances find it hard to enjoy their relationship because so much time and effort is extended toward the psychological trauma and struggle. At this point it doesn't matter which came first—psychological problems and then marital problems, or vice versa. If someone has severe psychological deterioration, those individual problems must be addressed before healing can come to the marriage.

2. *Numbness.* The lack of empathy for a mate is very common in unhealthy marriages; numbness exists. It is as if someone has given such people a shot of relationship anesthetic, and they are numbed as a result. They feel neither love nor hate; instead, they feel nothing. This is a very deteriorated position in marriage. Many times I have heard, "I think he is a nice person and I really don't want to hurt him. However, I don't love him and I need to go on with my life." As a counselor it is much easier to deal with negative emotions than it is with someone who is numb.

3. *Victimized.* People in unhealthy marriages often feel victimized. It's easy to believe that the other partner is getting the best part of the deal, particularly in Active-Passive and Helper-Helpee relationships. These people rehearse all the occasions when they feel they were taken advantage of by their partner. They're convinced that if only the partner would change a few behavior patterns, the marriage would be better.

The focus of their mental agenda is on the other party rather than on themselves.

Along with that victimized feeling is an exaggerated level of sensitivity, which we often see in Active-Resistant and Macho marriages. Individuals take the behavior and words of their partner far too seriously. Every word, facial expression, and experience makes them feel threatened, abused, or perhaps abandoned by their partner. This exaggerated sensitivity can lead to a complete lack of trust (paranoia). Some people suspect that their partner is literally out to destroy them. A man might see his wife at the bank and think, "She never goes to the bank. After our fights over money, I bet she's cleaning out our joint savings account."

4. *Fantasizing.* Another serious detour in a marriage is when one or both partners privately fantasize about being single and/or being attached to someone other than their mate. When fantasizers hear about somone getting a divorce, they become jealous and think even more about what it would be like to be free from the constraints of marriage. They spend more time thinking about how to get out of the marriage than how to live successfully in it.

In addition, they may fantasize about a relationship with another person, whether it be a friend or casual acquaintance. This kind of mental unfaithfulness is often disastrous. Not only is it dishoneset, but it is not reality. When one imagines another person, he usually focuses on her strengths and then compares them to his partner's weaknesses. This can further discourage him from being actively involved in the marriage relationship. The fantasizer has lost hope that his partner will change in a specific area (weight, sexual prowess, vocational ability) which he feels is absolutely necessary for a happy, fulfilling relationship.

Fantasizers make a serious mistake by expecting fulfillment from their mates or another person. True and lasting fulfillment comes only through a relationship with Christ. Knowing and acting on this allows the couple to face reality and work constructively on their marriage.

Besides relationship and personal issues, there are at least three external factors that can detour a marriage.

External Factors

1. *Excessive involvement of friends and family in the marriage.* Chronic problem-filled marriages often lure other people to take sides. Friends, neighbors, or church members get recruited by each partner in order to reinforce his or her position, and so the couple is further divided. He has convinced his friends and acquaintances that she is at fault, and she has convinced her friends and acquaintances that he is at fault. The "friends," through their gossip and personal opinions, fan the flames between the couple, so that even if the husband and wife want to reconcile, it may be difficult.

Unfortunately, some communities and neighborhoods are vultures when it comes to the pain of a married couple. Unhealthy marriages serve as local soap operas for the public, providing them with entertainment and gossip material. This may sound bizarre, but many people get a kick out of another person's pain. If a wife decides to try to resolve the difficulties in her marriage, she can be ridiculed by her friends for attempting such an "absurd" move.

The only way to avoid this problem is to talk with only one or two close friends who will support you as a couple. When large numbers of people know, it is disruptive to marital reconciliation.

2. *Murphy's Law syndrome.* It seems that for some couples what can go wrong will go wrong. Upheaval may come from lack of job stability, financial insecurity, or difficulties with kids or extended family. One child may be sick in the hospital while another is having troubles in school. Dad cannot keep a steady job, and unemployment checks do not cover the family budget needs, so Mom has to work.

It is not that a couple invites life problems—they just seem to happen. Unfortunately, these put pressure on the marriage. There are well-established correlations between extended unemployment and divorce. The death of a child often causes marital upheaval and divorce. This should remind us that what "Murphy's Law" couples need is not our advice, but help in getting through their crises. This is not to say that these folks haven't contributed to their problems. However, they deal with a reality of life that others never know, and they need support, not criticism.

3. *Financial stress.* Sometimes too much money is just as damaging to a marriage as too little. The materialistic lure of fame or fortune can grab one or both partners. Their priorities center on what they can achieve or possess, and that becomes more important than the marriage. Other couples are just trying to survive. They wonder where the next meal is coming from or how to recover from bankruptcy.

Some marriages face a never-ending tension between a compulsive spender and a paranoid saver. One says, "You have to enjoy life" while the other says, "That's why I want to save now so I can enjoy it later." All of these produce financial stress, and can be destructive to a relationship unless a couple has a solid commitment to each other and the skills to work through their problems. While no marriage is immune from this pressure, Active-Resistant and Active-Active couples usually have better control of this area than other personalities.

Summary

A few detours are common in every marriage, and the three broad categories we've examined are certainly not a complete listing. But when eight or ten or more symptoms are present, you have serious marital difficulties.

So the question becomes "Can unhealthy marriages be cured?" Certainly! Just as healthy marriages can deteriorate because partners stop doing the things that keep a marriage healthy, so unhealthy marriages can improve when partners determine to work together to resolve their differences. It begins by realizing that God uses problems to help us mature.

While the apostle Paul was not writing about marriage when he confronted his "thorn in the flesh," we can use his insights to show how to deal with marital problems. In 2 Corinthians 12:7-10 Paul acknowledged that he had a problem that buffeted him. It was his human reasoning that informed God that he would be a better servant if he didn't have this "thorn." In the same way, we can honestly tell God that we feel we would be better servants for Christ if we didn't have some of our marital problems.

However, Paul discovered that eliminating his problems was not the answer. Paul made a significant statement when he said that he had learned to be content with his weakness, because "When I am weak, then I am strong." Paul learned that his very weakness introduced him to the strength of Christ. Likewise, I believe that when an individual or couple have difficulties in their marriage, that very weakness can introduce them to Christ's strength, which will ultimately strengthen their marriage relationship. Unfortunately, many individuals short-circuit that power by complaining about their problems rather than receiving God's help.

Where do you begin? First, jointly identify your marriage personality. (Remember—you're not choosing what personality you want, but recognizing what your personality already is.) Second, review this chapter and Chapter 2 to pick out healthy and unhealthy behaviors that are true of your marriage. Third, take the Marital Assessment Questionnaire found in the Appendix. This will help you evaluate your marriage.

Once you've identified the strengths of your marriage, make a conscious effort to continue them. Then pick out one or two weaknesses that are easier to work on, and design a plan for improving them. If you work on a couple of problem areas and then experience success, this is far more productive than rehearsing all your problems at the same time.

Major Problems in Marriage

As you evaluate your marriage through the first 11 chapters and the Marital Assessment Questionnaire, you will probably identify one or more root problems. We're not talking about the fruit on the marital tree, but the roots that produce the fruit. We're going to look at such things as dependency, self-orientation, family of origin, and communication (where most marital problems originate). It is my desire that you can find positive solutions in these basic root issues so that, no matter what your marriage personality, you can experience a healthier marriage.

It is impossible for me to escape the comment of James 1:2-4: "Consider it all joy, my brethren, when you encounter various trials; knowing that the testing of your faith produces endurance. And let endurance have its perfect result, that you may be perfect and complete, lacking in nothing.'' As you read the rest of this book, remember that problems are opportunities for personal growth. Don't be afraid to confront your problems. God can and will use them for your benefit.

CHAPTER 12

Overcoming Dependency

One of the most traumatic events in the life of a baby is when his pacifier is taken away from him. Screaming, yelling, pleading, begging, tears, and pathetic facial expressions are all part of his guilt-producing routine that says, "How could you be so cruel, so unsympathetic, so uncaring?" Eventually, after a few rough nights, the child discovers that he can live without that pacifier. There's no hard rule about when it is appropriate for a child to stop using a pacifier, but it must happen someday. A six-year-old sucking on his pacifier in first grade would seem out of place.

While weaning a child from dependency on a pacifier is an obvious responsibility of parents, we are often not so diligent in other areas. Too many permissive parents don't allow their children the privilege of developing a sense of identity and personal confidence. Others are so protective that their children grow up without learning how to deal with life issues. This makes them dependent on their parents, society, or other individuals. Often that person is their mate.

By dependency, I mean a condition of leaning on other people because of a lack of personal self-sufficiency. Dependency is transferring responsibility for our own lives to other people. It's blaming others for our own unhappiness. It's feeling intimidated by other people. It's obstinately declaring that we don't need others, though underneath we really do. It's constantly deferring to other people's opinions in order to be accepted. It's overdepending on others for our happiness and underdepending on ourselves.

Dependency should not be confused with low self-esteem, which has to do with how I value myself as an individual.

Dependency is a close cousin, but it reflects the view I have of my abilities and talents to handle life on my own. There are many talented people who secretly struggle with low self-esteem. The dependent person may accept himself, but he feels inadequate in dealing with life's situations.

The reason dependency is such a problem is that the true source of happiness is not our environment or our marriage, but our peace with God and our contentment in walking with Him. In marriage it is appropriate for us to lean and depend on our partner to some degree. That is part of intimacy and closeness. However, when two individuals constantly lean on each other, or one leans too heavily on his partner, that becomes a hindrance to the marriage relationship. One partner is drawing life from the other rather than giving to that person. Marriage is designed to be a shared partnership, and it works best when two people feel confident and capable to live on their own.

Lighting a "unity candle" in wedding ceremonies is symbolic of two individuals becoming unified in marriage. However, many people confuse marriage *oneness* with marriage *sameness*. They think that being one means thinking the same, feeling the same, and acting the same. Their goal in marriage is to be one in all areas of life.

When unity is achieved in marriage by sacrificing individuality, there is no longer a healthy marriage. For example, a husband and wife have only superficial unity if they agree with each other because they are afraid to disagree. A woman might not tell her spouse how she feels because she believes he will be offended. A steady diet of this behavior is a frustration to her and the relationship. She feels she is being dishonest, and he doesn't benefit from her input. Both lose.

Sources

In order to address the problem of dependency in a marriage, it helps to realize why we feel dependent. The major source of dependency is found in the family of origin. In some cases, children have no role models in their parents. Others have no guidelines to follow. The parents may have lacked internal peace or felt like failures in life, so their children experience embarrassment and/or a lack of security.

Dependency also develops when parents are overly critical. When a child is always told what he is doing wrong, that child doesn't gain much confidence. A child who grows up in an atmosphere of constant complaining about insignificant issues will feel inadequate. It may be reflected in poor performance in school or sports or in peer relationships. A child who does not have a place to "park himself" in the sense of feeling good about who he is and what he does feels in constant need of other people. Relying on others can be expressed in an excessive need for advice, hostility toward peers (the hostile person is simply covering up feelings of inadequacy), or avoidance of contact.

Signs of Dependency

Two statements are constant refrains among people who visit my office: "Unless he changes, there is no way I can live with him" and "I just can't live without her. I don't know what I would do." In the first statement, the person is saying that she is dependent on her partner's behavior for happiness and fulfillment. The second statement is a more obvious reflection of dependence. He is also saying that he is dependent upon her for his happiness and fulfillment. Both have the wrong focus, for genuine contentment comes only by depending on Jesus Christ.

Sometimes it is difficult to recognize when we're overdepending on our spouse. There are at least four signs that should warn us of this condition. The first is when we have difficulty accepting the differences in our spouse. He may be of a different political party, like different food, have different values with regard to money and socializing, or view child discipline from a different perspective. Our goal should not be to change our spouse, but rather to study him in order to understand him.

A second evidence of dependency is overcompensating or overprotecting a weakness or inadequacy in the spouse. Susan is a good example. She feels fairly confident and capable, and at the same time she wants to help her husband. He has trouble managing their household finances, so when a few unexpected bills come in, she knows that he will be upset and will worry about having enough money to pay those bills. So she takes care of the problem without saying anything to him.

Occasionally such action might be appropriate, but as a regular habit, this is a sign of weakness. Making him dependent on her indicates that she does not respect him. Susan is actually hindering her husband's development by not letting him learn to deal with money as a responsible adult. Also, she may begin to feel frustrated by the ongoing problem and distance herself from him emotionally.

Anger is a third evidence of dependency, especially in the Helper-Helpee (by either partner) and Active-Passive (by the active partner) marriages. This anger is the result of anxiety—the need to have things turn out a certain way in the marriage. It's reflected in loss of temper, nagging, or chronic complaining about the spouse's lack of responsibility.

Finally, a very common symptom of dependency is a feeling of being crowded or smothered. Smothering happens when the dependent person is either unwilling or afraid to make decisions on his own and is constantly asking for advice from his partner. This includes simple things like unwillingness to confirm any social engagement without checking with the partner or lack of freedom to make a 20-dollar purchase. If something goes wrong at work or at home, there is an immediate need to consult with the nondependent partner for advice and support. There are varying degrees to which the nondependent person feels smothered, but this goes on to some degree in many relationships.

Dealing with Dependency

The key to solving the dependency problem is realizing that each person is responsible for who he or she is. *That does not change after marriage.* We still have responsibility for ourselves, but now we have an additional responsibility—to support and aid the growth of our partner.

A few years ago my wife gave me a special card that emphasizes this truth: "Your heart is my heart. Your truth is my truth. Your feeling is my feeling. But the real strength of our love is that we share rather than control each other's lives."

Sharing instead of depending—that's the goal! It's two people, each with unique insights and abilities, giving to each other for their mutual benefit. Let's examine how this happens.

The first step is learning how to be content. I cannot escape the impact of Paul's statement in Philippians 4:11: "Not that I speak from want; for I have learned to be content in whatever circumstances I am." Note that Paul said he *learned* to be content, which implies that it was not automatic and that it required some time.

Contentment in this verse implies self-sufficiency. It is not self-sufficiency based solely upon self, but based upon a confidence in God and self. The reason Paul could be content in any circumstance was because his circumstances did not intimidate him—and remember that Paul was in jail when he made this statement. The reason circumstances did not intimidate him was because he was confident in himself and his relationship with Christ. He wasn't being obnoxious or presumptuous or overly confident, for over a period of years he had experienced enough successful situations involving his initiative and God's intervention so that no matter what happened it would be for his good and God's glory.

Self-sufficiency does not automatically happen for most of us. It is a learned behavior developed when we experiment with life and try to push the boundaries of what we perceive to be our personal limitations. Certainly marital upheaval is one setting where we are forced to push the boundaries.

Contentment and self-sufficiency go hand-in-hand with self-respect. If I am going to develop self-respect I must start by recognizing how God sees me as an individual. There is no doubt that you are a treasure in God's eyes. Many people feel uncomfortable with that statement, but it is true. We are highly valued by God because He has created each of us as unique expressions of Himself. It takes faith to begin to treasure ourselves as God treasures us.

One way to see why God values you, and consequently why you are important, is to identify your strengths, hobbies, wishes, and values. Some of you may not feel comfortable with these recommendations. However, if you struggle with dependency, no one else can solve that problem for you. The reason you need to identify your strengths is so that you can have an accurate assessment of the qualities and gifts that God has invested in you. Then your responsibility is to allow yourself, and God through you, to demonstrate those positive traits to other people. In this way you gain a fuller appreciation of God's work in your life, and your dignity as an important person in God's eyes increases.

For best results, take a stack of three-by-five cards and list at least 10 to 15 personal strengths—one per card. What do I mean by strengths? A strength is anything you do well in terms of vocation, habit, or hobby, and also positive personality traits, such as listening, cooperation, and tolerance. Many people have problems listing even three or four strengths. Force yourself to identify at least ten. At the beginning of each day, review your 10 to 15 strengths and select one to mentally focus on during that day.

Another helpful exercise is to compliment yourself on your strengths. You might say something like, "Charles, you really do have some capabilities and talents. You're not only a good tennis player but you also have some tremendous mathematical skills. You are a good cook, and you help your wife keep the house clean. Another strength I like is your organizational skill." The mental conversation goes on until you have completed the list of strengths.

You may feel uncomfortable doing this, but it is very important. You may think, "This is too much focus on me as an individual," but it isn't. You are recognizing your strengths and acknowledging the fact that God, in creating you as an individual, has planted within you certain capabilities and strengths. You must recognize these in order to use them, in your marriage as well as in your whole life, to bring glory to God. Another way to do this is to make your recitation a prayer: "Lord, thank You for giving me the ability to work well with children." Then review all your qualities, recognizing that they are given to you to use for His glory.

Most individuals spend too much time rehearsing their weaknesses while ignoring their strengths. They spend all their energy trying to identify what is bad without identifying and developing what is good. Often the best way to deal with weaknesses is to compensate by focusing on our strengths. The truth is that we aren't going to rid ourselves of all our weaknesses. But by using our strengths we are freed to work on our weaknesses, one at a time.

In addition to identifying your strengths, it is important for you to identify some hobbies. This addresses the question "What are you doing to enjoy life?" An important part of living life is pursuing some enjoyable activities. This helps bring necessary breathing room into our everyday pressure-filled existence.

Next, write a wish list. This list should have 20 things that you would like to do in your lifetime. They can be ridiculous or very practical. For example, you might wish to climb Mount Everest, or you might wish to buy a new car. You might desire to be a missionary, or you might want to win the ball game next week. The wish list has no limitations in terms of money, size, location, or personnel. Its purpose is to allow you to dream, to break out of your limited perspective, to gain a glimpse of what you can accomplish through God's power.

Finally, you need to list what you believe in. Write down your values. What is important to you in being a spouse? What does it mean to be a responsible worker, a responsible citizen, a responsible Christian, and a responsible parent? Most of us have these values, but often we aren't conscious of them. Identifying them allows us to know what we believe and why, so that our actions become a reflection of these values.

Identifying your strengths and focusing on them, and identifying your hobbies, wish list, and beliefs, will give you a better understanding of who you are and can lead you to personal appreciation. The more we appreciate and respect ourselves, the less dependent we are in our relationships. This allows us to move away from feeling that we *need* other people to feeling that we can *enjoy* other people.

One way to enjoy people and become less dependent is to take more initiative in social situations. Some people find it easy to avoid conversing with others, and instead to depend on people to approach them. But the person who is gaining self-respect is willing to take some risks.

The principle is similar in marriage: It is important for the dependent spouse to practice making more decisions. Before seeking the advice of a spouse, think through the situation yourself and try to reach your own conclusion. This process may be aided by recognizing your strengths, hobbies, wish list, and values.

The benefit of this process is that it allows you to stop blaming your partner for the problems in your marriage. If you want to feel victimized by your partner for the rest of your life, you can—but it will destroy you and your relationship.

Realize that feeling victimized is usually a reflection of your feelings of inadequacy and dependency. It is a mistaken belief that you are powerless to do anything about your situation. You are not powerless. As Paul learned to be content in all situations, so can we. Contentment doesn't mean accepting everything; it means feeling self-sufficient, able to deal with any circumstance. One of the best ways to deal with a struggling marriage relationship is to reduce the focus on your spouse and how he or she may have taken advantage of you. Instead, focus on your own strengths and dreams and values, seeing how you can be more completely developed as an individual created by God. This will ultimately be of great benefit to your marriage.

Dependency and Marriage Personalities

Because dependency is an individual condition, it is evident in all seven marriage personalities. The degree of dependency affects the strength and/or weakness of every marriage relationship. However, the problem of dependency is most clearly seen in Active-Passive and Helper-Helpee marriages. Because of this fact, I want to make some specific suggestions for those two marriage personalities.

In the Active-Passive marriage, it is very important that the active spouse recognize her dependency. The reason she wants him to change is not so much for his good but for hers. The more pressure she puts on the passive partner, the more he tends to withdraw, which makes her frustrated.

Instead of attacking and blaming, the active partner should confess her feelings of frustration. Here's an example: "John, I appreciate the fact that you say you will clean up the dishes while I go to the meeting. However, it really bothers me when you promise to do something and then I come home and it's not done. I'm tempted to be upset, but I think it's better to tell you how I feel and leave it at that."

If the passive partner doesn't respond, the next time she might say, "I was disappointed last time when you promised to wash the dishes and you didn't. I would like some clarification. Do you want to clean up the dishes while I'm gone at the meeting, or do you not? I'm not so concerned whether you say yes or no, but if you do say yes, I would like for it to be done, and if you say no, then I won't expect it to be done. It's really up to you." Notice that while she is honestly communicating her feelings, she is not depending on her partner to make her happy.

The passive partner must also recognize that he has a dependency problem. His natural desire is to avoid conflict, and so he depends on his spouse to carry the responsibility of the relationship. This is not a healthy way to live. It affects us physically with symptoms like high blood pressure, and it affects us emotionally, producing feelings of guilt, fear of failure, and self-doubt.

The solution is for the passive partner to take some risks and become more active. He has expected life to be easy, but it is not always that way. To gain the benefit of a happy marriage, he needs to honestly confront his partner, perhaps saying something like, "Helen, I find it very difficult to talk to you, but I'm going to risk it. I want you to hear me out before you say anything."

Another evidence of the passive person's dependency is his expectation that people accept him the way he is. To some degree that is valid, but it can be used as a manipulative ploy to not grow. It is important that you see that God's acceptance of you is complete, but an expression of that acceptance of yourself is to allow God to continue to move you beyond where you are toward maturity in Christ.

The Helper-Helpee marriage demonstrates unhealthy dependency, as we've seen earlier. In a sense, the helpee depends on the helper in much the same way as a child depends on its parents. But the helper is dependent too, for often the reason he helps is for his own benefit rather than for the good of his spouse.

The helper must recognize that when he continues to aid in the helpee's shortcomings, he actually makes his partner feel inadequate. He is really *not* helping. Suppose Denise is afraid to drive—though she has a license and is a capable driver—and doesn't like large groups. She depends on her husband, Dave, to drive her around town and to be with her at meetings. Dave, the helper, might actually help Denise by saying, "Honey, I love you, but I will not take you to your meeting tonight. You can drive to the meeting by yourself. I realize there are several people there who bother you, but you can handle it. I will support you and pray for you, but I will not do it for you. I care for you too much to let you continue to suffer like this.''

The helpee can become less dependent by putting a little distance between herself and the helper. One way to do this is to engage a close, trusted, responsible friend as an occasional adviser. This will remove some of the pressure in the marriage relationship. It is important that the helpee begin to inform the helper, and then act, instead of relying on the helper to act on her behalf.

Evidence of Progress

You know there is less dependency in a relationship when a partner feels less smothered, or when there are fewer expectations and the husband and wife are more tolerant of their differences. As a matter of fact, those differences may even become interesting and attractive. One of the most significant evidences of reduced dependency is when a couple experiences more freedom to talk with each other without complaining or withdrawing.

Dependency, in my opinion, is the most predominant problem in marriages today. It is the result of a growing deterioration of individual responsibility and sense of worth in our culture. We have become dependent upon government, neighbors, and friends to live our lives rather than depending upon our own personal character, worth, and value as individuals. If this is the case in your marriage, recognize it as God's open invitation for you to become more like the person that God intends for you to be. This will work in your relationship, for people who feel content and self-sufficient are better able to truly love their spouse.

CHAPTER 13

Healthy Self-Orientation

Self-orientation is a problem of overattention on self that is expressed in two very different ways. One extreme is commonly known as the egotist. His self-orientation is overt as he pushes for his own way, thinks he is the greatest, and aggressively expresses his superiority. The other extreme is low self-esteem. This self-orientation is covert, consisting of feelings of inferiority and of a person not getting his own way.

There must be balance between loving ourselves as God loves us and loving other people. The apostle Paul expresses that balance well: "Do nothing from selfishness or empty conceit, but with humility of mind let each of you regard one another as more important than himself; do not merely look out for your own personal interests, but also for the interests of others" (Philippians 2:3,4).

Excessive self-focus, whether expressed as egotism or low self-esteem, is a serious problem in many marriages. Let's examine each and see what steps can be taken to correct the problem.

Egotism

Egotism could best be described by the word "narcissism," which simply means an excessive interest in one's own appearance, comfort, status, skills, and character. Its roots are in the Greek legend of Narcissus, a beautiful young man who was so cocky that he refused all offers of love. As punishment for his indifference, he was made to fall in love with his own image in a mountain pool. Unable to possess his image, he wasted away until the only memory of his existence was a flower that bears his name.

Like Narcissus, egotistic people draw excessive attention to themselves. They feel compelled to put others down in order to prove their greatness. Their commitment is not to others but to themselves. They don't depend on others for survival; they can make it on their own. They do not blend well with other people, unless those individuals see life from their perspective. They insist that their point of view is always right.

Egotists have a tough time in marriage. Their interests tend to be in outside activities, such as job and hobbies, rather than in the home. This doesn't mean that they don't care about the marriage, but rather that they derive more fulfillment from their accomplishments than from their relationships.

The most obvious example of egotism is Mr. Macho in the Macho marriage. Most Active-Resistant marriages also have an egotistic partner in the resistant role. I have occasionally told egocentric partners that they are a lot like a rock in a blender. To them, anyone who does not fit in with their plans is a source of irritation.

The egotist has several fears which influence his lack of trust for people. He fears that he is not as significant as he would like to believe. He fears that he is not as independent as he would like to believe. And he greatly fears being controlled by other people. To him, being vulnerable to someone is being controlled. He is afraid that his vulnerability will be used against him, so he resists closeness even though, in many cases, he truly desires it. He cannot imagine divulging his future, feelings, thoughts, and goals to another person. Even though his fears are misguided, it is very difficult to convince him otherwise. The only person he ends up trusting is himself.

Recommendations

If you recognize that you are self-focused, one of the best things you can do is realize that it's not your nature to be warm and affectionate and caring. However, your spouse still needs your affirmation. You can compensate for your weakness by "scheduling" compliments and affirming actions such as special cards, flowers, and other forms of recognition.

Yes, this takes practice. So put a reminder on a three-by-five card at work or else at home in some place where the other spouse can't see it. Then while you're driving, or during a break in your day, identify behavior that you appreciate and rehearse an appropriate compliment to give your spouse. Then schedule when you will do it, and follow through on it. If you do this enough times, you may begin to feel like doing it, and it will become more natural.

It is also important for you to be right. Have you considered that you can sometimes be right by admitting you're not right? This means that you don't always have to know the right answer. You need to risk not always being in control. Though you do not often make mistakes, when you do it is extremely important that you take the opportunity to admit your error instead of making an excuse or blaming someone else for it. Yes, this is risky, because you believe your spouse will take advantage of you or make fun of your error. But in reality he will probably respect you more and you will have a stronger relationship.

It is important to experiment in small ways with trusting other people. For example, you might give your children some chores. After giving them your instructions, let them do the chores without any intervention from you. Then compliment them for what they did well, even if you must suggest some improvements.

The same is true for your spouse. You are afraid that she would not accept you if she knew the real you. The only way to find out is to take a risk and experiment with letting her know the real you. Jesus Christ is our model in this. First Peter 2:23 describes Christ prior to His crucifixion: "While being reviled, He did not revile in return; while suffering, He uttered no threats, but kept entrusting Himself to Him who judges righteously."

By entrusting yourself to God and to other people, you can effectively reduce some of your defensiveness and resistance to other people. Follow Christ's example when you are disappointed in your spouse, your children, or your friends. Instead of following your natural inclination to write them off, go the second mile. Give them another chance. Take some more risks. Though it's difficult, you will benefit by developing and becoming more productive as a person.

For those who live with an egotist, I have two recommendations. The first is the most difficult: Do not personalize his behavior. It is tempting to misinterpret lack of trust, distance, and pushiness as disloyalty and rejection. The self-focused person may provide things for you and perform duties to prove his love, and you will feel that this is insincere. Realize that he feels incompetent in interpersonal relationships and that this is his way of trying to compensate. If you can accept his attempts to demonstrate love, this will encourage him to do more, and in time it may become natural.

The second piece of advice may sound contradictory. The egotistic person has difficulty trusting and risking in interpersonal relationships. So instead of pushing him to be close and to share his personal thoughts and feelings, do just the opposite. If you happen to be married to a workaholic husband, encourage him to work more. The less you try to rope him in, the more he will feel a freedom to draw closer to you.

I realize you may be protesting, "I desperately need a close, affectionate relationship, but I'm not getting it with this egotist. How can I push him further? Don't I deserve a close relationship?" I agree that you should have a close relationship with your spouse, but you are much more likely to accomplish some degree of intimacy if you don't actively demand that your partner draw close to you. Pushing, arguing, complaining, and nagging will only drive him farther away. So why not try this approach, and give him some time to come to you?

Low Self-Esteem

One of the fun experiences at a carnival is the "House of Mirrors," where participants can see themselves in several different ways. One mirror may create the effect that a person is tall and skinny with a wiggle in the middle. Another mirror may show a person to be short and squatty with an oblong head. In both cases, the person's image is determined by the mirror he looks at.

In a similar way, parents are a "house of mirrors" for their children. A child's self-image is based on how he perceives others see him. The image is created by facial expressions, tone of voice, positive and negative feedback, patience or impatience, and general mannerisms.

Children are nonverbal experts and they "read" parents like a book. They desperately want and need approval from their parents, and if they subconsciously believe they are unacceptable, their self-image is distorted. They aren't mature enough to recognize that a parent can make mistakes or have a bad day. If Dad is irritable, it may be because of pressure at work or unusually heavy rush-hour traffic. But a child thinks it is his fault. If a parent doesn't explain the difference, and consistently criticizes the child and puts him down and tells him he is no good, the child is gradually programmed to believe that he is of little value. Even when he is an adult, this can have a definite negative effect on his marriage.

When I suspect this problem, I ask a person to tell me what he likes about himself. He is usually very uncomfortable; it would be much simpler if he could tell me what he does *not* like. His worth and value are not based upon internal personal worth, but on his external performance. He may actually be very successful in business or sports, but it isn't enough. He feels he has to be perfect to make up for his internally-felt shortcomings.

A woman with low self-image often approaches marriage on the basis of what she can get rather than on what she wants. She doesn't believe she can commandeer the individual who will fulfill her dreams, so she compromises. After all, if she doesn't feel good about herself, why should anyone else? If low self-esteem is acute, she may even think she doesn't deserve to be happy or successful. Then she may find it extremely uncomfortable to let other people love her because she doesn't love herself.

Recommendations

Probably the biggest challenge for people with low self-esteem is to begin to approve of themselves. The thought of liking themselves without condition seems overwhelming initially, but it can be accomplished. Also, these people need to allow others to love, approve, and affirm them—just as they are. When given a compliment, they need to learn to say "Thank you" instead of explaining away the accomplishment or the performance.

It's important to remember that valuing myself is my

responsibility. As a creation of God, I'm to be responsible to God as a good steward, and that includes viewing myself as God sees me. One of the best ways to confront low self-esteem is to literally accept all that we are, including the strengths and weaknesses. The person who rehearses only his weaknesses and denies his strengths is like a person swimming upstream in the midst of a flood. He can swim and swim and swim until he is literally dead tired, but at best he will only have stayed in the same place.

Let's examine again the example of Paul in 2 Corinthians 12:9,10: "He has said to me, 'My grace is sufficient for you, for power is perfected in weakness.' Most gladly, therefore, I will rather boast about my weaknesses, that the power of Christ may dwell in me. Therefore I am well content with weaknesses, with insults, with distresses, with persecutions, with difficulties, for Christ's sake; for when I am weak, then I am strong." Note that Paul discovered a very important secret to his success in life. He accepted his weaknesses as from God, and in the process they became the very source of his strength because they forced him to depend on Christ. The same is true for us. The person who recognizes his weaknesses is positioned to be used in a significant way by God. And that can raise your self-esteem!

The specific tools for dealing with low self-esteem are very similar to the ones recommended for dealing with dependency. I recommend that you do the exercises suggested in the previous chapter. Put your strengths on three-by-five cards and review them regularly. Identify your values and write a wish list. As you see your strengths and kindle your vision, you will begin to value yourself as a significant individual created by God.

Low self-esteem and egotism can be an issue in any marriage. However, the conditions are most evident in the Active-Resistant, Macho, and Kids' personalities. In a Kids' marriage, both partners need outside mentors to help them overcome their immaturity and low sense of worth. The other two personalities can often make improvements on their own. Let's look at them separately.

The Active-Resistant Marriage

The active partner often struggles with low self-esteem and seeks approval and affirmation from the resistant one, who responds with intimidation and hurt. The result is distancing and criticism. The more the active partner demands affirmation, the more he pushes the resistant partner away. One way to solve this problem is to observe how to catch butterflies. Often the best way is not continually chasing them, but standing still. When the butterfly feels safe, it often flies near you, and you can snatch it.

Chasing your resistant spouse sets up your own rejection, which reinforces your subconscious fear that you are not worthwhile. So stand still and leave room for the resistant one to come back into the relationship. Don't place heavy demands upon him. At the same time, get involved in your own activities. Gradually the resistant partner will begin to feel it's safe to move closer in the relationship. Admittedly, this may not seem fair or very appealing to the active partner, but it usually works.

The Macho Marriage

Mr. Macho's outward show of strength covers an internally felt weakness. His harshness, irritability, and insensitive personality push people away. Their rejection confirms that he must not be worthwhile. He often rationalizes the rejection, thinking that people reject him because he is mean, which covers up a greater subconscious fear that people reject him because he isn't worth much. That's why it is so difficult for him to be accepting, caring, and sensitive. If he adopted that behavior and people still rejected him, it would be a harsh blow to his pride. He subconsciously doesn't believe he could handle that result.

One of the best ways for Mr. Macho to correct this condition is to realize that he is going to be rejected in life, and to accept this fact. Rejection happens to everyone, deserved or not, and it's not all that bad. When Mr. Macho is put down or made fun of, but accepts it and realizes that it is not the end of the world, this reinforces his sense of self-esteem. He has confronted something that he has feared for years and dealt with it successfully.

Mr. Macho needs to stop demanding of people and instead start requesting. When he begins to *ask* for things instead of demanding them, he runs the risk of people not complying.

But he benefits in that when people do comply, they think more highly of him—which reinforces his sense of worth. In addition, it is important that he give compliments to his wife and other family members, and express gentle affection for other people with strong handshakes, pats on the back, hugs, and facial expressions that communicate approval.

How does Mrs. Macho, who also suffers from low self-esteem, deal with herself and her spouse? She has become so used to her "plight in life" that she continually reaffirms her low self-esteem. It is most important that she get on a "high-protein diet" of self-affirmation. She needs to find a responsible, caring, and insightful mentor—someone other than her husband—such as a close friend, counselor, or objective acquaintance.

Her new self-respect starts at home with her husband. When he makes a demand on her, it is important that she stand up to him in a positive manner. It can be cooperative, but on her own terms. She benefits both of them in the process, for it does not develop his self-worth when he gets away with pushing people around.

Though it may sound impossible, one of the best ways to deal with the surface anger and gruffness of Mr. Macho is through humor. Smile at him and say, "I wish you could see yourself in the mirror when you get gruff like that. You look like an old gray bear! You might try lightening up a little. You never know, you might like it!" Humor is a great method for removing tension in a relationship.

It is important to recognize that self-orientation, whether reflected in egotism or low self-esteem, is usually a reflection of childhood family experiences. So to progress in this area, it will also be necessary to come to grips with your family of origin. And that requires another chapter.

CHAPTER 14

Resolving Family-of-Origin Issues

Thanksgiving and Christmas are special times when families reunite, share life experiences, and enjoy one another. So why does my counseling load increase significantly at this time of the year? The people who come into my office are not anticipating fun and relaxation; they're dreading the tension and stress. Unresolved emotions and conflicts with parents and siblings that may lie dormant much of the year resurface before and during these gatherings.

It's important that we examine the family of origin—a person's parents, brothers, and sisters—because it has a significant effect on the health and personality of a marriage relationship. I find very few people who have not, at one time or another, had to work through feelings about their family. Often that processing of emotions does not take place until after a marriage is consummated. We cannot escape our past when we move into marriage. Our experiences affect how we view all of life—career, family relationships, and our own attitude toward God.

Marriage and family expert Dr. James L. Framo has stated that the best single prediction of how a marriage is going to turn out is based on the quality of family one comes from and the kind of marriage one's parents have. While it is not impossible to have a better marriage relationship than your parents, it is not easy.

A good marriage is not automatic, but is influenced by experiences during childhood. There are at least three ways in which the families of origin affect the stability and health of a marriage: in blending two family backgrounds; in dealing with negative emotions, traumatic events, and behavior

135

patterns; and in postmarital involvement between a couple and their families of origin. Let's examine each one of these.

Blending Two Backgrounds

Family relationships defy understanding. Family therapists can identify communication patterns, but they do not understand how families have developed those behavior patterns and why they continue.

When two people marry, they face a challenge somewhat like climbing Mount Everest! They must begin to understand each other's family backgrounds, blend those backgrounds together, and develop their own way of relating. They must work through such areas as how to express affection, ways of expressing anger, vocational attitudes, discipline of children, vacation values, relating to extended family, spiritual understanding, work ethics, living conditions, and attitudes toward money. The challenge of blending increases in proportion to the difference in backgrounds and the strength of the personalities.

It takes a minimum of six to eighteen months for newlyweds to get through the "rumblings" of the adjusting and adapting process. Some tremors seem strong enough to register on the Richter scale. One spouse may have grown up in a family where disagreement and raised voices were virtually unknown; they either avoided conflict or dealt with it in a quiet manner. The other spouse may come from a home where complaints, criticism, and heated confrontation were common. These two people will struggle in the blending process because their negotiation styles are dramatically different.

If a couple in the first six months of marriage finds it difficult to deal with issues, they should consult a third party for help. During the first year or so of marriage, most individuals are motivated to work on their relationship because they have strong feelings of care and love. They should take advantage of those feelings and develop skills to deal with their differences, keeping in mind that their goal is not to change the other person but to make adjustments to each other.

Negative Emotions and Traumatic Events

Someone has said that life is a journey in which we are forever leaving home. One never escapes his childhood, but usually (over a period of time) is able to put those childhood experiences into perspective. However, some family experiences are so deeply ingrained in us that they negatively affect our marriage relationship. In fact most marriage dysfunction has a family-of-origin component. A person dealing with childhood family hurts is psychologically caught between his family and his spouse. The diagram demonstrates what I mean: The person is neither fully in the marriage nor fully in the family.

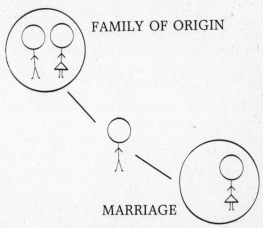

This person may seem involved in everyday marriage functioning, but mentally and emotionally he is captivated, trying to understand, resolve, and put away the past. He is unable to fully attach himself emotionally to his spouse.

Let's examine several ways in which your family of origin may negatively influence you and hinder your ability to function in marriage.

1. *Traumatic events.* In my office some patients literally fall apart when they talk about the events of their childhood. Some of their stories are horrifying: beaten with a board; forced to go on a milk route at three every morning; memories of a drunken father beating his wife. These are real-life experiences that leave deep emotional scars. For some people the trauma is not nearly as dramatic, but still very painful. They may have suffered with constant criticism or condemnation from parents or siblings. Others face a continuing mental replay of a father or mother's mean scowl of rejection.

I visited with one woman who hated her father and never wanted to see him again. Yet he had an incurable disease and she was obligated to visit him. As far as she was concerned, the sooner he died the better, for he had repeatedly beaten her and her siblings unmercifully. She was angry and bitter toward God, wondering how He could have allowed such a man to be a father. The trauma of her childhood spilled into her marriage. She could not trust anyone on an intimate level because she was deathly afraid of being hurt again. Her family had taught her that closeness was painful. Before she could begin to trust her husband, she had to resolve the bitterness toward her father.

2. _Guilt_. Some people feel guilt because of their parents' actions. It's very common for children to blame themselves for the breakup of their parents' marriage, thinking that if they had not been around, maybe their parents would have made it. This thinking is often subconscious, and of course misguided, but it's still very real.

Another source of guilt occurs when parents have regularly complained, criticized, or condemned the behavior of a child. No matter what the child does, he hears about it. Consequently he assumes a "my-fault" syndrome and finds it difficult to feel like he deserves much in life. This person finds it difficult to escape the mental tape recordings that he hears from Dad or Mom. He's "fat," "ugly," "dumb," "a klutz," or "shy." He was told such things as "You'll never amount to anything" and "The world would be a safer place if they didn't let you drive." He may go so far as to feel anxious and uncomfortable if things are going well for him. The adult who feels guilty because of constant criticism from parents during his childhood often sabotages his marriage by treating himself and/or his wife with an unending stream of criticism, just like he received from Mom and Dad.

If you were fed a continual diet of rejection, you may have established the habit of self-judging, in which you constantly evaluate and condemn your own behavior. You have faithfully adopted your parents' critical pattern, and now you treat yourself the same way they treated you. This guilt affects your marriage in two ways. First, self-criticism can so diminish your self-worth that you can't see how your spouse can love you.

Consequently, you discourage closeness and teamwork by not allowing yourself to be a full-fledged partner in the relationship. Second, a guilty person may take up this habit with the spouse, acting out his own frustration by inflicting wounds of criticism, complaint, and condemnation.

3. _Lack of acceptance._ Children desperately want approval from their parents. Some children are so anxious to be accepted that they perform in every way possible in order to earn recognition. They do what is expected and more.

Of course the compliant, performing child in most cases garners acceptance and affirmation from parents. Parents love to raise an easy child, especially one who also does well socially, academically, and athletically. However, a very subtle psychological mindset can develop in which the child gets the idea that he is worthwhile, and people will accept him, only as long as he performs.

After a while he begins to subtly and overtly resent that pressure. His resentment may grow until he reacts by breaking out of the bonds of marriage and away from what is expected of him in society. People in the community are shocked because this was a person who was always dependable and responsible—a model citizen.

Lack of acceptance can negatively affect a marriage. A person may be unable to accept genuine love from the spouse because she does not believe that she is lovable. She may even set up her partner to reject her by distancing herself as a test of the spouse's genuine love. This individual needs to learn that she is worthwhile, in and of herself, whether or not she performs. Unfortunately, this is not easy to do, and the spouse can't do a lot to help. She needs a third party, someone with whom she is not connected and for whom she does not need to perform. This person—perhaps a pastor or marriage counselor—can help her see her value and can help her work through her self-condemnation.

4. _Hurt._ Most parents, because they are so busy providing for their children and dealing with their married partner, have trouble always being sensitive to their children. Occasional hurt is a predictable part of family life. However, ongoing deep hurt

can result in shattered lives, with people seeking security and not able to find it.

Adults who have been deeply hurt as children tend to approach life apologetically instead of assertively. One young woman told me, "The only positive family memory I have is dancing around the room one Christmas with my grandfather and he said that he really liked me." The rest of her life was full of memories of family violence and being so scared at times that she would go into her closet and stand there shaking until the fights were over.

Hurt also comes from feeling ignored. One man said the only positive memory of his dad was a walk they took together one Sunday afternoon. Most of his childhood he felt like an unwanted child. This deep hurt has to be resolved or he can never truly open up to a wife. One way this man helped to resolve it was by writing a letter to his father, even though he was deceased, and expressing his feelings as well as his desire to forgive.

5. _Overprotection_. Marriages are often disrupted because the partners were overprotected while growing up. Overprotected children usually struggle with personal confidence. So much has been done for them that they don't realize what they can do for themselves. There is lurking, subconscious anxiety that undercuts their confidence in decision-making and interpersonal relationships. Overprotectionism does not allow a child to reap the consequences of his behavior, and this destroys his dignity and sense of worth.

An adult who has grown up under persistent overprotectionism may seek advice on the simplest of decisions, and even avoid decisions entirely because of fear of failure or of making the wrong decision. Such indecisiveness breeds unrest in most marriages because the partner cannot count on him. This condition often affects the Active-Passive, and the Helper-Helpee, and to some degree the Kids' marriage personalities.

6. _Closeness Anxiety_. A couple with whom I counseled both had alcoholic parents. During one interview the husband was asked to create a metaphor to describe his marriage relationship. He saw his marriage as one in which both of them were floating around in space, each encased in a plastic cylinder.

They could see each other and communicate nonverbally. However, though they were reaching out to each other, they could not touch because of their impenetrable plastic shields.

This is a powerful symbolic statement of a condition called "closeness anxiety." This occurs when someone wants to be close to the spouse but at the same time is desperately afraid of being close. This anxiety comes from two directions: A person is anxious because she is afraid she will not be close enough, and she is also anxious because she is afraid she may get too close and be hurt. This is extremely common in children of alcoholic marriages, though it is not unique to them. Closeness anxiety is almost always found in the Active-Resistant, Macho, and Pretense marriages, and sometimes in the Kids' marriage as well.

As a result of their negative family experiences, many adults carry mental burdens that weigh them down and rob them of a truly happy marriage. Resentment is one such mental burden: Bitterness imprisons and distorts healthy feelings. Some people take on a second mental burden—a vow that they will never be like the parent or parents that they hate. A vow like that inhibits their freedom to be who they are. They end up living with a negative perspective, trying not to be like someone instead of trying to reach their full potential.

A third burden is that of unanswered questions: "Why did my dad abuse me, and why did he never apologize or even acknowledge what he did to me?" Why certain things happened and why they were allowed to happen can create so much mental anguish that an individual struggles with feeling secure in a marriage.

Finally, there is the burden of carrying family secrets. You know something that no one else knows, but there is no way that the secret can be revealed because of the negative impact on other people. Therefore you continue to carry the burden alone. This is especially common among victims of incest.

These burdens can plague people for years. I know of individuals who avoid graveyards where family members are buried. Also, certain sights and smells remind them of negative events in the family. Other people suffer recurring nightmares about abuse from a sibling or parent. No one likes being imprisoned by these mental burdens, yet they persist.

Unfortunately, we cannot change our past, and it is useless to continue to fix blame because that won't change history or relieve the burdens.

Recommendations

The first thing you need to do is recognize that your parents wanted the best for you. You may react at this point and protest that I do not understand your mom or dad. That's no doubt true, yet there are very few parents who do not ultimately want the best for their children. Unfortunately, many parents who want the best also do some horrible things, and I am not trying to excuse their behavior. Instead, it is extremely important that we recognize that our parents were programmed by their parents. They were parenting the way they were taught, according to the model they had in their homes.

Also, it is important to recognize that parents are going through other life issues of which the children are often unaware. Such things as unemployment, marital discord, unpaid bills, and poor physical health can trigger abusive behavior. You can accept the strong possibility that your parents do care for you and desire the best, or you can fight it. It's your choice. However, refusing to accept that fact continues the mental suffering for you, not for them.

In order to relieve those burdens, identify some of your life difficulties that are family-related. You might review items one through six and then add any others you think of. Write them down, identifying a few specific instances from your past that illustrate your hurt. Then ask yourself, "Am I bitter or resentful toward my parents? Am I still trying to please my parents? Are there some unanswered questions that I would like to have cleared up?" List as many items as you can, as accurately as you can.

It is a clear mandate in Scripture to confess wrong attitudes. If we are bitter or resentful, we need to clear the deck of those negative emotions. Giving them over to God will not erase all the memories or all the feelings associated with these memories, but it can serve to release us from their burden so that we can go on with life. Some issues that you struggle with are not a matter of being wrong before God. You were hurt through no fault of your own. I suggest that you express your feelings of hurt and your unanswered questions to God. Better yet, write them down and read them to God. If necessary, find a caring witness to help you in this process.

The next step is to consider the possibility of confessing your negative attitudes to your parent(s). The Scripture indicates that confession of our sin to one to whom we have been embittered is necessary, according to Matthew 5:23,24. However, there are many extenuating circumstances which may complicate this for you. You simply may not be able to find it within yourself to approach your parent, no matter how convinced you are that the Scripture is correct. You can approach God and tell Him, but it hurts too much to face your parents. A second potential complication is that your parents may not be approachable. They may be in ill health, or the relationship between you may be such that they refuse to talk to you.

If you do talk to your parents, first make an appropriate confession of your wrong attitudes. Then express disappointments, hurts, and other concerns that you had as a child. This is not a "dump" session, but an updating for the purpose of improving your relationship. But be careful. If you have difficulty handling this encounter by yourself, bring a sibling, a close friend, or your spouse.

If a personal encounter is not possible or reasonable, then consider sending a letter or a cassette tape and request a response. If a parent is deceased, I often recommend that a person write a letter to the deceased parent, expressing some of his frustrations, needs, and hurts. It might also help to go to the parent's gravesite and talk to him or her there.

Sometimes memories of the family of origin are so painful that there is no way to even think about them. The mental images are like a chamber of horrors that gnash at you and try to render you emotionally immobile. Your only defense is to try to avoid them completely. But that doesn't solve your problem. You need to be free from that hurt, and this may require a professional therapist, a pastor, or a close and mature Christian friend. You need a witness who can accept the truth as you experienced it, and then declare the truth from the biblical perspective. This person can accept your pain and at the same time announce the healing of God.

As an adult it is important to recognize that you may never

get what you really want from your parents, whether it's recognition, approval, an inheritance, or even a heritage. You need to accept that fact, surrender your expectations, and accept the reality of the relationship with your parents as it is. This doesn't mean that it can never change, and certainly you should hope and pray for that. But you can't depend on the situation changing, because it may not.

Though none of us would ask for pain as a source of growth and personal development, it often serves that purpose. You might take some time to write down the advantages of your painful childhood and adolescent experiences. "What advantages?" you ask. Well, often the very negative events of our lives help mold and influence us in positive ways. For example, I know individuals who have a tremendous sensitivity to hurting children and adults because of the negative experiences of their own childhood. They are able to comfort and help these people because they understand the pain and have worked through it themselves.

Your character, life goals, values, beliefs, and motivation have been positively influenced by some of your negative experiences. Certainly there are struggles because of your family experience, but that is not all bad. If you begin to recognize the fact that those negative experiences have been used and can continue to be used for ultimate good, it helps reconnect you with life. You will benefit, and so will your marriage relationship.

Family-of-Origin Involvement

We've examined two ways that family of origin affects a marriage—in the blending of backgrounds and in the emotional pain caused by traumatic events in childhood. Our final area is the involvement of parents and in-laws in the marriage. Balance is the key word here. It is healthy neither for parents to be overinvolved in a marriage nor for there to be no active relationship with them at all.

Our family dog, Brandy, is an illustration of the balance we need. In four different pregnancies she produced 24 puppies. As soon as each pup was born, it wanted to nurse. For the first two or three weeks, our Brandy was fairly cooperative, but after awhile nursing those demanding puppies got rather old.

After six weeks she'd had enough—no more nursing. The pups whimpered, desperately searching for a warm breast full of milk. It was hard for our kids to hear the whining, but they soon forgot after watching the playful pups slurp up baby cereal. By quitting, Brandy actually helped her pups take off on their own.

The Bible says in Genesis 2:24, "For this cause a man shall leave his father and his mother, and shall cleave to his wife; and they shall become one flesh." The text clearly states that part of marriage involves leaving the family of origin so that one can cleave or bond to his marriage partner. Many marital difficulties are the result of one or both partners not leaving their family of origin. Their parents are always available when they need money, a listening ear, or a refuge in times of marital strife. Or the parents continue to impose themselves on the couple with unsolicited advice, unrealistic expectations, or excessive gifts or financial support.

It is important for both sets of parents to "cut the umbilical cord" as they watch their children marry. This is not always easy, especially if parents are overinvolved in their children's lives because of their own dysfunctional marriage. Their marriage stays alive as long as they're busy working with their children. When their children no longer allow that assistance, the parents have to face each other, and that can be disconcerting.

Sometimes parents have invested too much in the success of their children. They have dreamed for years that their child will be a college graduate, or succeed in a certain profession, or parent their grandchildren in just the right way. So Mom and Dad continue to focus on their children, even after the children are married, trying as hard as they can to position their children for success and comfort in life. In so doing, they continue to "nurse" their children instead of allowing their children to learn how to feed themselves.

A related problem is when parents are disappointed in their child's spouse, and exclude the spouse from the family, except for special occasions such as Christmas and birthdays. This kind of behavior often creates jealousy, hard feelings, and divisiveness in the marriage. When parents side with their child against the child's spouse, it's almost a sure way of driving the marriage closer to divorce court.

Recommendations

When dealing with the family of origin, there is one cardinal rule: <u>Each person deals with his or her own parents.</u> The daughter is going to understand her parents better than her husband, and her parents are likely to be more responsive to her. If the son-in-law attempts to run interference for his wife, it will disrupt her relationship with her parents. Another reason why this rule is important is what I call the <u>"family under-standing"</u> that exists between children and parents. There are a few exceptions to this rule, but in most situations it works the best.

When overinvolvement with the family of origin is recognized, there needs to be some disassociation. It is important for couples to disassociate from their parents, not because they dislike them, but because it is the only way to deal with their addictive dependence on Mom and Dad. Occasionally if a child does not do this and the parents are aware of the dependency, then they must initiate action. This is not always pleasant, and it can be anxiety-producing, but it is necessary.

How do you go about the separation process? Sometimes geographic separation is required, especially if a couple and one or both parents live in the same community. When the distance between the two families is increased, there will not be the expectation to spend as much time together. There is no magic to geographic separation, but sometimes it does help.

If geographic separation can't take place, reduced social contact should be considered. This means that the couple should go beyond their parents for some of their socializing. The idea is to broaden their base. All of us learn from our social contacts, and if we limit those contacts, we limit our personal development, including our spiritual life.

It may also be necessary to approach the parents with some specific issues of concern. If parents are constantly questioning the couple's financial decisions, parenting behavior, social relationships, or domestic skills, the blood-related child should confront his or her parents with their overinvolving behavior and politely ask them to back off. For example, a wife might say something like this: "Mom and Dad, you know that I care for you and I want the very best for our relationship. However, my husband and I feel that at times you are still correcting and advising to excess. We appreciate the interest that you express in us and want that to continue. But at the same time, we need to be treated as adults. So please allow us to make our own decisions, and only give us advice when we ask for it."

Sometimes the parents may have to initiate action by telling their child that they have been presumed upon too much and that the couple needs to make it on their own.

It's not easy to deal with Mom and Dad and family-of-origin issues. Most people love their parents and don't want to hurt them. And parents don't want to hurt their children. Sometimes it's as if the children are out on the playing field of life and the parents are in the stands. The parents are clapping for their children and shouting occasional advice. However, couples must fight their own battles, and as they do they will gain self-respect and dignity, and there will be more respect between the parents and the child.

CHAPTER 15

Understanding and Preventing Affairs

Affairs are certainly not an easy subject to discuss, but a necessary one. Hardly a day goes by that I don't have to deal with this issue in counseling. The stories change but the theme remains the same—discouragement in marriage leads to affiliation with someone else.

As I approach this subject, I experience two contradictory feelings. On the one hand, I recognize the pain of so many people. Yet I also remember the restoration of so many marriages as a result of this devastating experience. As a matter of fact, I've become convinced that out of the very depth of despair marriages can be resurrected so that they are stronger than if the affair had not occurred. This is not to imply that we should encourage affairs. But if an affair has happened, we must approach it with the belief that the end result will be a better marriage.

Let's look at the story of Bob and Karen to see how an affair develops. This couple married when they were teenagers. At that time Bob was a laborer trying to keep bread on the table for his young wife and children, which eventually numbered five. He was aggressive, young, and hungry. He learned quickly, and after a few years he decided to start his own business. Hard work—six days a week and sometimes a seventh day—led to that financial security he had always desired. He bought a newer home, two cars, a microwave oven, and all the other modern conveniences a family could desire.

But Karen didn't share the joy of his success. She became more and more disheartened with the burden of raising five children with virtually no help from Bob. She was separated from her extended family and felt very alone, having little contact with the outside world besides trips to the grocery store and occasional visits with a neighbor. At times she succumbed to periods of depression and required medication to keep functioning.

It certainly was not premeditated, but one day a workman came to fix some plumbing. One conversation led to another conversation. For the first time in years she found herself talking to someone as an adult—and that someone was listening. She realized that she had not felt so peaceful in a long time. It was rewarding to think that someone was actually interested in what she had to say and listened without walking out the door in the middle of a thought to go to another job site. An affair was the natural result.

Bob came unglued when he found out. He thought he had done everything he could for his wife by providing a home and financial security, and her thanks was a kick in the face. He experienced feelings of rage, anxiety, and deep hurt. He also felt like a fool, and also guilty, realizing that he must have played some role in his wife's behavior. For days he was in shock, feeling numb and rejected. His bitterness intensified day after day until it reached almost unmanageable proportions.

At times Karen felt guilty too, yet she defended her actions. She knew it was not right, but at the same time it felt so good. She was a lonely person who needed some attention, and that attention came in the wrong way.

Affairs Defined

As you read about this marriage, you probably took sides. You may have found yourself sympathizing with Karen and her loneliness, thinking, "It serves him right for ignoring her all the time." Or you may have felt sorry for Bob because he tried to satisfy his family and was treated unfairly. But it does no good to take sides in this kind of situation, because both partners contributed to the dysfunction of the marriage. And both of them need to work through this if they want to reconcile their marriage.

Bob and Karen are now on the road to a happy marriage. Karen's affair was not the end of the world. But first they had to answer a critical question: Did they want to move on in the marriage and resolve their problems, or was this affair going to control their future? This was a decision that only the two of them could make, and they decided to move forward in their marriage, making the necessary changes.

The first step was for Bob and Karen to understand that an affair is a redefining of the marriage structure by shifting the primary loyalty away from the marriage partner. Most people think of an affair as an illicit sexual relationship. By that definition they fail to realize that Bob also had an affair. No, he did not have a relationship with another woman, but he shifted his primary loyalty away from Karen to his business. It is possible to have a primary loyalty for your children apart from your spouse. Or you can give primary loyalty to your job, church, volunteer activities, hobbies, or friends. Anytime our mental agenda and activities are devoted to a person, activity, or thing that takes priority over our spouse, then in the very strict sense of the word we are involved in an affair, for it infringes upon the exclusiveness of the marriage.

Affairs are a fact of life, whether we like it or not. The vocational marketplace in the last 20 years has escalated the contact between men and women—secretary with boss and professional-to-professional relationships. The very freedom of movement that men and women enjoy, along with unhappiness at home, are the chemistry of affairs. The attitude of our society does not help. Sexual promiscuity and extracurricular marital involvement are accepted in many circles and serve as entertainment for many people. Even those who won't actively pursue an affair can be jealous of those who do, for they can identify with their own unhappy marriage relationship and long for something more exciting.

Affairs take place because a spouse is dissatisfied with the marriage vacuum and is desperate for closeness and affirmation. When people are not receiving what they truly need and deeply want, they are tempted to look for it elsewhere. Sometimes an affair is a reaction to what the partner has or has not done, or even a payback for an affair. It can be a form of escape, such as when someone is married to a very dependent person. Many people enter an affair by sharing their problems; it feels good to be heard and understood and cared for by another person. That's what happened to Sam.

Sam had always been "Mr. Right." His dad was respected

in the community, with a successful business and involvement in many volunteer activities. Sam wanted to be like his father and consequently was very compliant with the demands and rules of his family. He went to the right school, got the right grades, performed in the right ways, and went to the right church.

When Sam married Jennifer, everyone thought she was perfect for him. They had children and became established in the community. However, eventually he realized he was not happy. Every decision he had ever made was based upon what was best for other people. He had never made a decision just for himself, and he had lost touch with who he was as a person.

This craving need to be his own person set him up for a relationship with Tanya. She listened as he talked about his life, and seemed to understand that he really cared for his wife and children, but also felt a sense of emptiness in his obligation to them. She empathized as he talked about how he both loved his father yet couldn't stand him. He felt trapped, wanting his father's approval but also wanting to live his own life and make his own decisions.

Tanya's ability to listen "hooked" Sam into the trap of an affair. She too benefited from the arrangement because she did not respect her own husband. Sam was aggressive, successful, and financially secure, the opposite of her spouse. She needed him because she wanted to move forward in life, and he needed her because he wanted to choose something to please himself without regard for other people.

Sam feels terribly guilty about his unfaithfulness. Jennifer has always supported him, and he feels obligated to her and really doesn't want to leave the security of that relationship. Yet he has strong feelings for Tanya. She seems to understand him more than anybody else, but he doesn't realize that this is mainly because he has talked more to her about his true inner feelings than he has to anyone else.

Critical First Steps

What should Sam do? Should he do what he knows is right or should he do what he wants to do? The problem with doing what is right is that he has always done what is right, and he is sick and tired of doing what other people expect of him. The problem with doing what he wants to do is that he knows it is wrong and will probably not succeed.

No one can make that decision for Sam. But I can assure him that if he chooses to do what is right, and is willing to be patient, he can gain new feelings for his wife, Jennifer.

If you have been or presently are involved in an affair, let me tell you what I told Sam and Jennifer, and Bob and Karen. First of all, the reason you were involved is due to tension in your marriage relationship. However, it is important to recognize that an affair is not on solid ground. You can't depend on an affair developing into a permanent relationship. Marriages consummated out of affairs do very poorly because the cornerstone of an affair is a dysfunctional marriage. Do not be fooled by the ecstasy of feelings and enthusiasm for this relationship. They are temporary and in most cases cannot stand the test of time. Attempts at breaking up one marriage to enter another are usually wrenching experiences that leave husband and wife decimated. Financial stress, bitterness, and problems with parents and children all assault the new marriage, destroying it as well.

Most of the time an affair is an unconscious expression of desperation by the affairing person. They are in an affair not because they want to get out of a marriage, but because they cannot live with their marriage the way it is. An affair seems the only way to motivate themselves and their spouse to get help. This is usually not a premeditated effort on the part of a person involved in an affair. But subconsciously the message being sent is, "I do not like the marriage the way it is, and I would like some improvement."

Another critical point is the necessity for the affairing person to let go of the affair. You cannot resurrect a marriage relationship with split loyalty. A choice must be made, and that choice is sometimes extremely difficult.

If you are the spouse of an affairing partner, you need to realize a few important facts. First, affairs do not break marriages; affairs come from broken marriages. The marriage was broken in the sense that it was not sufficiently meeting the needs of at least one partner. Individuals who are happy in their marriages rarely become involved with a third party.

An unhappy, unfulfilled partner is vulnerable to the affair auction block.

Realize also that affairs are rarely unilateral: They're bilateral. If your spouse has had an affair, or is having an affair, then probably you have also had or are having an affair. This may sound offensive, but stick with me for a moment. Remember our definition. Affairs are not only with *people*, but also with activities, hobbies, and other family members. The offended spouse, often unintentionally, has become too involved outside the primary loyalty to the partner. Two typical situations are a mother who becomes so focused on her children that she forgets her husband, and a husband who is so enthralled with his job that he ignores his wife. When the offended spouse appears disinterested, it gives subconscious permission for the affairing spouse to step out of the marriage. Consequently, both the offended spouse and the affairing partner bear joint responsibility for the marital breakdown. For your own good, do not allow yourself to place exclusive blame on the affairing person, because this will only further harm the marriage.

A third point is to remember that when you get beyond your hurt, there is great hope. This affair will test your commitment to marriage. Are you truly committed to your spouse for better, for worse, for richer, for poorer, in sickness, in health, till death do you part? Or are you committed only as long as it does not infringe on your comfort? There is great hope in this situation because it forces two people to focus on their relationship more than they have in years.

Remember the fire alarm going off when you were in elementary school? That fire alarm was so powerful that it motivated everyone to attention and action. An affair is a fire alarm to a marriage relationship. It motivates people to reconstruct their marriage. In the long run they may be better off than some of their friends who have drifted into a "so-so" relationship, but are not motivated to work on their marriage. This couple can be thankful, even though it has taken some deep hurt, that they are motivated to pursue a mutually fulfilling and supportive relationship.

Tips on Reconstruction

When an affair is discovered, it is usually much more

productive for the couple to solicit the aid of a third party, particularly someone who understands marriage relationships and how they function. The initial stage, from my point of view, is management. This couple needs to be "quarantined" so that the tremendous emotional strain is restricted within a circle of protection. If either or both of the partners begins to talk about this situation to a number of other people, the chances that the marriage won't survive increase significantly.

The less people know about an affair, the better. Unfortunately, when an affair becomes public knowledge, sides are taken, gossip spreads, and the couple becomes local entertainment. People feel free to give advice that the couple doesn't need. It's best to keep the problem to themselves and to trust only one or two confidential parties. This will make it easier to work through the pain and agony of this marital difficulty.

Management also recognizes that there is an initial shockwave, and that time is needed for settling. It recognizes that both parties are hurting, but in different ways. The victim feels offended and used and abused. The victimizer—the affairing person—feels trapped between obligation to a marriage and romantic attraction to another party. Both husband and wife need time to work through their hurt, and to express their feelings either individually and/or together in therapy.

It is important that the offended party not be allowed to threaten or issue ultimatums to the affairing partner. Ultimatums are an attempt by the offended party to try to reestablish a sense of security, but they rarely work. The offended party needs to learn to trust in a relationship with Christ, not in promises by the spouse.

Remember that the issue is not the third party; the issue is the couple's relationship. Constantly discussing the "whys," "hows," and "whens" of an affair only irritate the marriage; they don't improve it. If the offended partner harbors feelings of resentment, and attacks and questions the affairing partner, that sabotages the reconstructive process. Obviously the offended partner undergoes severe anxiety and questioning, but it is best to talk about it with the marriage therapist.

Management also means that the affairing spouse needs to regain confidence that the marriage relationship can work. Once he or she gains some of that confidence, there is more motivation to put energy into the marriage and to work on the relationship with some degree of comfort.

The management stage lasts anywhere from two weeks to two or three months, and sometimes longer. The next stage is the work and commitment stage. After a couple has dealt with their initial emotions, they need to start working on the areas of the relationship that led to the affair. By this point, even though there's still pain, a couple realizes that the affair is simply a symptom of their marriage difficulties. Their efforts need to be extended not in promising one another that there will never be another affair—though that is important—but in working to strengthen the relationship so that it becomes a source of fulfillment.

The problems identified in therapy will be addressed and worked through in this stage. This effort can last anywhere from two months to a year. This couple does not necessarily need counseling every week, but oversight by a caring professional during this time will be helpful, even if they only see the therapist once a month or so.

It is also important to realize that each partner needs time for healing. Two months to one year is normal, but occasionally it takes as long as two years. It is a mistake to think that only the offended spouse is experiencing pain. Both partners, in different ways, need emotional, psychological, and spiritual healing. Each experiences guilt, loss, despair, tension, and frustration. Neither has a corner on the emotional doldrums.

Trust is a major issue, and rebuilding it is a tricky task. The offended spouse has been deceived and now expects the affairing party to prove trustworthy. Bob felt he had to check on Karen, and was hesitant at times to believe her. Though understandable, this pattern doesn't work well. Bob has to learn to trust in God rather than in Karen's behavior. Though it was Karen's affair, and she needs to keep a straight course for herself and her husband, she cannot be expected to answer all his suspicions. Bob has to learn that the ointment for his emotional pain is developing a personal strength and security in Christ, then giving of himself to his wife so that trust will be rebuilt over time. Karen must also learn to trust again, giving herself to the marriage apart from the third party. She must believe that this marriage can work, and that it will not return to the ho-hum relationship of the past.

Remember that if a couple can handle this volatile situation successfully, they are establishing a relationship that is far stronger than previously. It is somewhat like a broken bone that becomes stronger than ever when it heals. The couple will have experienced some of the most difficult emotions in life and will have learned through them how to deal more successfully and honestly with each other. That becomes an important source of marital fulfillment.

I am convinced that this very difficult and heartwrenching experience can be turned to ultimate good. I have seen it happen over and over again. I would never encourage an affair, just as one would never encourage an accident, but affairs do happen and must be dealt with when they occur. Understanding why and how an affair took place can help two people handle it appropriately so that it will yield the best results. It doesn't have to be the end; it could very well be the beginning of a much more rewarding relationship.

CHAPTER 16

When Separation
May Be Appropriate

In an athletic event, it's not unusual for a coach to call a time out when his team is struggling. This allows for regrouping and for evaluating what is happening on the field of play. When a coach calls a time out, he is not signaling the end of the game; he is asking for a brief intermission so his team can get their act together.

In the same way, some struggling marriages can benefit from a marital "time out." This may sound like a shocking statement from a marriage counselor. But keep in mind that my goal is stronger marriages, and sometimes the best thing possible for the long-term benefit of a relationship is a temporary separation—a time out.

The purpose of a separation is to allow each spouse to get a better handle on himself. Couples need to do this when, as much as they want the relationship, they have lost the ability to handle the relationship. They may be experiencing continued conflict, or one may feel totally numb and unable to express and cope with his deep inner hurt. The more they hurt each other, the closer they move toward dissolution.

Let me say again that the purpose of a temporary separation is to save the marriage. It's a time for couples to regain objectivity, to look in the mirror and recognize that they are participants in the conflict and need to take responsibility for their actions. It's a chance to develop themselves as individuals in order to give to each other. It's a training period, a time to "get back in shape" so they can handle the marriage relationship. This may involve evaluation of personal skills, needs, weaknesses, and failures. It allows time to read books about marriage and personal growth and to give special effort to spiritual exercise, including reactivation of a personal walk with God.

Separation is best when initiated by both parties, though usually one wants the separation more than the other. If one partner is really striving for separation, the other is wise to agree. When a separation is engineered, a third party (such as a pastor or counselor) needs to monitor the relationship. With the counselor, the couple must agree on their plan for being apart. The length of separation is usually one month to four months. However, they shouldn't try to determine the length of separation at the start.

While apart, the couple should have regular but limited contact—one or two telephone calls and one visit for a maximum of five hours per week. They should agree on how often the spouse living away from home will see the children. And they need an agenda for how they will use their time for personal growth and development. When a couple makes this kind of arrangement and fulfills it, then the separation usually has very beneficial results for the marriage.

I would encourage the spouse who may resist separation to be patient. Don't sacrifice your dignity by begging, pleading, attacking, or making suicidal threats. If your partner has left, let him go without hounding him. There is no guarantee that he will want to come back to the marriage relationship, but your chances are better when you allow him room to make his own choice for the marriage. You may feel a need to convince your spouse that you have changed. You may be tempted to use the argument, "We can't work on our marriage while we're separated." But this won't work. At this time, working on your marriage means working on yourself. If you want to guarantee the destruction of your marriage, then hound the person who has left, and he will probably make the separation permanent.

I realize that this takes great patience. But remember, you want your spouse to come back because he or she has chosen to, due to his or her own dignity and spiritual values, and not because of your pressure.

I have four suggestions for what each partner can do during the separation. First, it is important to do some reading. The reading should focus first on the Bible. Ask God to give insight and wisdom about you as an individual. Use the Scriptures not only as an instructor, but also as a source of encouragement and strength. It is also important to read some self-help books. Topics may include such areas as self-esteem, parenting tips, marriage relationship helps, and so on. Books serve as an objective input without requiring you to respond to a human being.

Second, it is important that you establish and maintain a relationship with a caring third party who is mature and objective, someone who exhibits God's wisdom as well as wisdom about life itself. Be sure that this person is not experiencing personal life difficulties at the time. It is more difficult for him to be objective if he is experiencing his own problems.

Third, involve yourself in a few projects or hobbies. This is not to keep yourself so busy that you never think or read, but to help you relax and feel good about yourself as an individual.

Finally, after you've been separated for a minimum of two weeks, it is important that you begin a process of self-evaluation. You need to ask yourself, "What kind of person am I? What have I done to contribute to this marital disarray?" You should look at your values regarding marriage and family life, and what you want for yourself as a Christian person in the long run. Hopefully, self-evaluation will help you face your strengths and weaknesses, then stimulate the process of further developing your strengths and allowing some adjustment to your weaknesses.

I am not suggesting that separation is the answer to every chronic marriage problem. It is not. I am suggesting that at times separation is the best avenue, especially when both parties desperately need a break from the action in order to recollect their thoughts and feelings. I have told many couples that a few months out of the entire length of a marriage is not that long—if used effectively for one or both partners to deal with themselves and reconnect in marriage.

CHAPTER 17

Negotiation Skills

Good communication alone does not make a marriage, but it is certainly evidence of a healthy, functioning relationship. Unfortunately, many couples are ill-equipped for effective communication, and this intensifies other marital problems. Without this necessary skill, it is much harder to keep two people together. Couples need to know how to effectively negotiate with each other. In this chapter we will examine the elements of effective communication and negotiation, and suggest some ways to accomplish this in your marriage. The first step in the process is learning to communicate who you are.

Speaking for Self

Someone has said that there are three kinds of responses in families—yes, no, and nothing. It is by far the most difficult to deal with the "nothing" response. The other person is left floating, with very little idea of what is going on in the partner's mind.

The first essential for effective communication in marriage is for each partner to be like a billboard. Billboards along busy streets and highways state a specific message: Use a certain bank, drink a particular soft drink, watch the local news program. The message is direct and clear, and it is my choice as to how I respond to it. Similarly, a couple needs to tell each other their message so they are not left guessing what the other thinks. Our job is to give our spouse messages about our beliefs, thoughts, and feelings. The purpose of this step is not to persuade, complain, or produce guilt, but to provide information. This is best accomplished by using "I" messages rather than "you" messages. "I" messages communicate my thoughts and feelings and imply responsibility for my own behavior. "You" messages communicate blame and avoid taking personal responsibility: "You always do..." "You should have..." "You never..."

In speaking for self, there are three levels of communication—what you want, how you feel, and what you think. A wife may say, "I would like to go out to dinner with you, but I feel a little afraid and embarrassed because I think it is improper to ask, since it's my birthday." Note that her declaration incorporates all three levels of communication. She could have said, "You forgot my birthday again!" or "You never take me out to eat. You even expect me to cook on my birthday!" But those statements put her husband on the defensive. By using "I" statements, she lets him know what she wants, feels, and thinks, but allows her husband to choose his response.

This form of communication shouldn't be carried to extremes. If you want the salt at the dinner table, it would be a bit ridiculous to say, "Dear, I want to tell you that I need the salt for my hamburger, but I feel embarrassed to ask you for it because it may interrupt your meal." However, on important issues, make sure you declare what you want, how you feel, and what you think. Suppose you need to discuss a situation with your spouse. You might say something like this: "Honey, there's something I need to discuss with you and I'm wondering when would be the best time to do it. It will probably take about five or ten minutes. We can do it now, if this is a good time, or later in the evening. When can we sit down and talk?" Use the same tone to tell your spouse what you think or want in specific, direct terms without trying to persuade, complain, or make him feel guilty.

It is not uncommon for someone to have little or no confidence as a communicator. I frequently hear comments like "I can't say it," "My words get all jumbled up," or "I get too upset." If you are not sure of yourself, try this kind of statement: "Honey, there is something I would like to tell you, but I really don't know how to get started or go about saying it. Would you sit down with me and let me ramble for a few minutes? You can listen to me and then tell me what you think I'm trying to say." Then don't worry about how you're communicating. Just tell your spouse what is going on inside you, and you may be surprised to find that your partner understands. If she doesn't, then let her ask some questions to try to clarify your thinking.

In our discussion of speaking for self, the partner must also be listening. That is the second important tool in communication. I like to call it "active listening."

Active Listening

Hardly anything a spouse does will communicate more love, respect, and caring to the partner than listening. One of the most important things I learned in graduate school was the significant change that takes place in a patient when a counselor actively listens, without giving advice or significant feedback. That's equally true for marriage relationships.

When I use the word "listening," I am thinking of more than just hearing another person's words. You need to be a student of your partner. That's why I call it "active listening": It's "tuning in" to another person in order to accurately hear what he is saying, both verbally and nonverbally. That's hard work! We must listen to the words but also observe inflection, tone of voice, and body language in an attempt to understand the message. Listening is often curtailed by a listener's defensiveness, lack of objectivity, or tendency to prejudge the message of the sender. It's easy to "turn off the ears" because you have "heard this before."

Here are four practical listening tips:

1) Stay within five feet of the speaker.
2) If you cannot listen, for whatever reason, agree on a time to talk about it later.
3) Do not interrupt.
4) When the speaker is finished, repeat back what you have heard and allow the speaker to agree that you understand or to explain further. If necessary, ask questions for clarification.

It really helps if the speaker knows you're listening. You can communicate by maintaining eye contact with your spouse, leaning forward, giving an occasional "uh-huh" or "please go on,'' and generally maintaining an open, attentive posture.

Let's see how this works with Ralph and Dottie. After dinner, Dottie approaches Ralph by saying, "Honey, I'd like to discuss our discipline of the children for a few minutes. Is now a good time, or should we set a time to talk later this evening?''

"Let's talk now," says Ralph.

Dottie sits next to Ralph, and they face each other. "Well, I've been concerned lately that the kids may be playing us against each other. I'm not sure that they know if we agree on what they can do and can't do, and when they'll be disciplined for disobeying.''

"In other words, you feel we need to spend some time discussing the rules and the consequences when they break those rules?'' says Ralph.

"That's right. I don't think we've done that.''

"Can you give me a recent example?''

Dottie can go on to give an example from that day's activities. Once Ralph understands the problem, the two of them can discuss a solution. This kind of conversation increases a couple's confidence in their relationship because they are treating each other with respect.

Conflict

Most people consider conflict a destructive force in marriage, but it doesn't have to be. In fact, proof of your negotiation skills comes in the arena of conflict. First, recognize anger as a helpful warning that one or both individuals are offended. It's a signal that something isn't working in the relationship, and that the couple needs to discover what is prompting the anger so that correction can be made. Let me emphasize that this anger is not out of control. Violent anger—throwing objects, physical abuse, or vicious swearing—is destructive, not constructive.

Usually anger is tied to one of three basic emotions—hurt, fear, or frustration. When someone is angry, it probably means that he or she has been bruised emotionally or physically, that he is afraid, or that he feels short-circuited in accomplishing a goal. If a couple can deal with the basic emotion that spawned the anger, it is healthy for the marriage. However, extended conflict that avoids dealing with hurt, fear, or frustration damages a relationship. The Bible shares some wisdom concerning this in Ephesians 4:26: "Be angry, and yet do not sin; do not let the sun go down on your anger." In other words, don't let anger accumulate, because it tends to turn into resentment and bitterness.

What steps can you take when you are angry? First, tell your partner that you are experiencing feelings of anger. If the anger is often volatile, it is critically important that you learn some procedures to interrupt that destructive habit. One suggestion is to give each other the power to suspend an argument simply by raising your hand. The termination of the argument allows each of you to cool off, reconsider your position, and then come back together with the sincere intention of resolving the disagreement.

Second, the intensity of conflict is often neutralized by moving closer to the person with whom you are angry. This may go against your natural inclination, but if you do it anyway, you'll generally find that the decibel level drops and the intensity of anger is reduced. People who hold hands or are within three feet of each other do not shout as loudly and tend to resolve their conflicts more quickly.

Now that we've established the essentials of speaking for self, listening aggressively, and maintaining the right attitudes in conflict, let's examine one effective method of negotiation.

The Bargain Table

The Bargain Table is a structured meeting arrangement between husband and wife. It is not unusual for one marriage partner to complain, "We don't talk enough" while the other concludes, "You talk too much." The Bargain Table is one way to help satisfy both concerns. Both partners agree to meet for a preset amount of time to discuss important issues in the marriage. This way, the one who wants to talk is guaranteed at least some conversation while the resistant one knows there is a time limit—usually 10 to 15 minutes. The Bargain Table serves to help a couple nurture a relationship, plan activities, and resolve conflict. Here are seven necessary ingredients for a successful Bargain Table.

Step One—*Time*. It is important to establish a *regular* time for the two of you to meet. It doesn't matter when you meet, but it is important to keep that time commitment without too many interruptions. If you agree to meet on Monday, Wednesday, and Friday evenings from 9:45 to 10:00, then each partner has the responsibility to be there on time without coercion.

Step 2—*Place*. Pick a place in which you will not be interrupted. If you are constantly answering the telephone or responding to children's needs, this will cause problems.

Step 3—*Position*. Sit in chairs facing each other, knee-to-knee and holding hands. This helps you focus on each other and be more efficient in your discussions.

Step 4—*Length*. Allow between 10 and 15 minutes. This may not seem like much time, but you will discover that it is usually enough to talk through issues, share goals for the week, or resolve conflicts. It is important that you not go beyond the allotted time, so that both of you can be more efficient and more motivated to stay on the topic.

Step 5—*Frequency*. I suggest a minimum of twice per week, up to a maximum of six times per week. It's best to start with two times.

Step 6—*Leader*. I recommend an even number of meeting times because it is important to alternate leadership. If a couple meets twice a week, the husband should lead the discussion one time and the wife the other time. It is the leader's responsibility to determine the topic(s) and lead the discussion. It is also the leader's responsibility to make sure that the Bargain Table begins and ends on time.

Step 7—*Format*. The first item on the agenda is an appreciation statement. Each tells the other one thing that he appreciates about his partner. Then the leader introduces a topic for discussion—perhaps something to resolve, plans for the future, or just information about the day. The listener actively listens to the leader, then repeats back what he or she hears the leader say. After the listener has parroted the message back to the leader, the listener can ask questions to clarify what the leader said or give an opinion about what has been presented.

Bargain Table and Conflict Resolution

The Bargain Table is an effective method for resolving conflict. If one spouse is upset, he or she can request a ten-minute Bargain Table, which should occur within the next 24 hours. The one who is upset is leader and presents the problem.

The listener parrots what is said so that the leader is assured that the listener really understands the situation. Sometimes the matter calls for confession and forgiveness by one or both partners. Occasionally you may need to work up a new agreement in a certain area. Conflict may also originate with a third party (child, employer, relative) and may need to be discussed between the couple so that each understands and agrees about what is to be done.

When using the Bargain Table to resolve conflict, it is important to stick to a limited amount of time, such as ten minutes. This requires the two of you stay on the topic. Conversations usually deteriorate rapidly if little progress is made in the first few minutes. Progress is measured partly by the attitude that each displays. You can tell if each of you is open and receptive, so that even if the issue isn't resolved the first time, the attitude leads to productive Bargain Tables in the future.

The Bargain Table will yield one of three outcomes when used as a conflict-resolving device: capitulation, compromise, or coexistence. Capitulation is one giving in to the other because that seems easier or more appropriate. Compromise means that the two of you give in to each other and reach a solution that is palatable to both. The third possibility is peaceful coexistence, in which both of you agree to disagree.

When a couple keeps butting heads over an issue, that irritates the relationship. It's like picking at a scab every day. The best thing to do is leave it alone and let it heal. Sometimes the best thing to do with a disagreement is leave it alone for awhile. Time allows two people to settle emotionally so they can have a more productive discussion on the topic at a later time.

Most people like to try a product before they buy it. Why not try the Bargain Table for two weeks and see how it works for you? If you find that it helps improve your communication and negotiation skills, then make it a regular part of your weekly schedule.

CHAPTER 18

Marital Goal-Setting

Most couples start their marriage with great intentions, and full of mutual enthusiasm, love, and caring. But gradually, in the course of pursuing their vocations, raising children, buying a home, and establishing financial security, they can lose touch with each other. It's not intentional or premeditated, but it happens.

This last chapter could be titled "Where Do We Go from Here?" Hopefully you've identified your marriage personality and perhaps seen some detours that have taken you off the path of a healthy marriage. Now it's time to make some adjustments.

There's an advertisement on television that shows an auto mechanic standing by an engine he has just repaired. He informs us that the owner of this engine will have to pay him $450. It's really too bad that this had to happen, because all the owner had to do was use a certain oil filter that cost $4.50. The mechanic then looks directly into the camera and says, "It's up to you. You can either pay me now, or you pay me later."

Goal-setting with your spouse is an excellent marital filter. Sure, some marriages require a complete overhaul. But for most it's a case of maintaining love and working to develop relationship skills so the marriage will flourish. Of course, you can choose not to nurture your marriage. But realize that you will reap what you sow. When we water and fertilize the seeds planted in a garden, we reap a good crop. If we do not nourish the garden, we will reap a limited crop, or no crop at all. Marriage relationships are no different: They respond and produce according to the amount of nourishment they receive on an ongoing, regular, daily basis. The choice is up to you.

Purpose of Marriage

If I were to ask you, "What is the purpose of your marriage?" what would you say? Most people don't have an answer. We think about how much we love or do not love our spouse and how things are going in our marriage, but most of us have not considered that the marriage should have a clearly defined purpose. What businessman would be so presumptuous as to walk into a bank and ask for 20 million dollars without a plan to use and pay back that money? Yet many of us go through marriage without any idea of where we have been, where we are, where we want to go, and how we're going to get there.

The following is a mission statement that one couple wrote for their marriage: "Our purpose is to grow in love for each other, support each other's endeavors, and serve God by using our gifts and skills." The purpose is long-lasting, but the activities involved in fulfilling the purpose change with time. Let me suggest that you write your own mission statement. By clearly defining your overall purpose in marriage, you are much better prepared to develop and execute your plans.

Planning

Many of us spend more time planning our weekly shopping list than we do our marriage relationship. When a couple knows the purpose of their marriage, it gives their relationship a sense of meaning and destiny. A plan puts shoe leather to their purpose. It increases enthusiasm for working hard and being involved in different activities. It encourages growth and establishes a sense of security because two people know that they are working together as a team to reach a common objective. Let's examine a process that will help you establish goals as a couple.

Goal-Setting Process

1. *Evaluation.* The first step in setting goals is to find out where you are. I suggest that a couple take a day or two and

get away from their routines. If you can, leave the kids and get away to a hotel. Take a calendar, an open mind, and an honest heart.

Start with a relationship evaluation. Each of you should separately write down your observations of the following:

Our Marriage Personality is _____

1) Strengths of the marriage

2) Strengths of yourself

3) Strengths of your children

4) Weaknesses of the marriage

5) Weaknesses of yourself

6) Weaknesses of your children

7) Needs in regard to relationship with extended family

8) Financial condition

9) Personal needs

10) Personal desires

11) Children's needs

12) Spiritual condition

13) Social needs

14) Social desires

15) Needs of your living environment

16) Vocational needs

17) Vocational desires

When you complete this exercise, compare your views with each other. This evaluation process should help you "locate" your marriage, identify individual and mutual concerns, and give you information to help you set goals. If you have trouble knowing where to start, you might take the Marital Assessment Questionnaire. The questions will help spark ideas.

2. *Goals.* What do you want to do with your marriage now that you have evaluated it? No, you can't quit! You need to establish one or more specific goals in five different categories:

1) Marriage

2) Family

3) Financial

4) Personal

5) Spiritual

Try to make your goals as specific as possible. Some goals for spiritual growth may be harder to measure than a financial goal to save 3000 dollars. To help give wings to those hard-to-measure goals, identify one or more activities that contribute to the goal. For example, the goal of spiritual growth might be clarified by church attendance, a daily prayer time, a summer conference, or personal study. All of these are measurable activities that will help you know if you are making progress toward the goal.

Marriage Goals: Marital goals should take into account interpersonal skills, the sexual relationship, time together, social activities, and educational or enrichment endeavors for the marriage. Identified marital weaknesses usually prompt a few goals. If the two of you are too busy, a goal might be to have four Bargain Tables per week plus three weekends away together during the year. If the two of you want to meet new people and develop a mutual hobby, you might decide to join a ski club.

Family Goals: Each child, based upon his or her strengths and weaknesses, should be discussed as far as social, academic, and physical development. Diet, education, extracurricular activities, and chores should be identified for each child. By doing this, each of you develops sensitivity to each of your children. Children feel, even subconsciously, your individual attention and concern. So cater your goals for each child to his or her individual needs.

An important area for you to consider is how you relate to your in-laws. If there are rough spots, talk about them and develop some creative solutions. Another important area is how you approach family devotions. Details concerning individual prayer time with the children and/or Bible devotions with the entire family should be determined.

Financial Goals: Assuming that a couple is married 30 years and has an average income of 25,000 dollars per year, they will go through 750,000 dollars during their marriage! Actually many couples go through much more than that. No matter how you cut it, that's a lot of money, and it is a good idea to manage it well.

I believe that money is rarely the major cause of a marital dissolution, but in many cases it is a constant companion to problems that face a couple. It's not simply a question of who pays the bills, but an overall approach to handling money. After you have reviewed your financial condition and established your goals, it is necessary to prepare a budget. In your budget, identify planned spending, giving, retirement, and investments. A budget should be structured for monthly spending and reviewed at least every six months. There are good tools available to help couples budget, and several are identified in the Appendix.

Personal Goals: To be a viable part of a marriage relationship you need to be a healthy individual yourself. So it's important to identify areas of need and interest on an individual basis. Share your interests, educational desires, hobbies, vocational drive, and any other personal needs with each other and see how you can support each other in accomplishing those personal goals.

Spiritual Goals: I have found that two people who are individually taking responsibility to maintain their intimacy with God have an increased capacity for intimacy with each other. People develop closeness with God in different ways. What's important is that you as a couple collaborate together on what works best for each of you. Some couples study the Bible well together, but most do it best on their own. Some couples fill their spiritual needs by being in a small group Bible study. Some find it difficult to discuss spiritual issues. For them, growth is best facilitated in a large Sunday school class or a church service rather than in a one-on-one format. When establishing spiritual goals for your marriage, examine ways to exercise your spiritual muscles. Spiritual vitality comes not only from receiving but also from giving, so discuss an avenue of ministry, such as teaching a Sunday school class, singing in the choir, or helping to feed the poor.

Activities

Once you have established goals in each category, determine activities to help you fulfill your goals. If you decided to save 3000 dollars, then figure out how you will do it. Maybe you will deduct a certain amount from each paycheck. Or maybe you need to get a part-time job. Identify all the activities necessary to accomplish each goal so that you can determine if it is realistic. If you can't achieve all your goals now, prioritize them so that you can accomplish the most important ones first.

Schedule

Planning is the easy part, since you can write down goals and activities for each of the five categories but never get them done. What makes all this work is a schedule. You will need two levels of schedule. First, write down your weekly routine —when each family member gets up, school and work times, when you have dinner, when each person goes to bed, and the other predictable, regular activities of each week. It's important not only for the husband and wife, but also for the children, to have some feeling for the routine of family life.

The second schedule is a monthly calendar to record all appointments and events that are not part of the weekly routine—vacations, visits to the in-laws, doctor appointments, recitals, church events, and so on.

Even if you follow through on part of what you originally planned, I believe the exercise of getting away, looking at the purpose of your marriage, evaluating your family life, and establishing goals and activities will help your relationship. Do not expect perfection the first time you do something like this. Healthy couples constantly make adjustments as they reexamine their marital goals and the needs of their relationship. But if you have some skeletal structure, then you have an idea of where you want to go in your marriage and why.

Of course, no one is going to make you set marital goals, but remember that the people who reap the most from a relationship are those who have sown the most in it. God has planted a treasure in your marriage. If you nurture it by evaluating your relationship, establishing proper goals, and then planning and scheduling activities to fulfill those goals, then get ready to reap more fully the bounty of God's treasure!

APPENDIX

Marital Assessment Questionnaire

This questionnaire is designed to evaluate the health of your marriage. Husband and wife should fill out separate questionnaires and then compare answers.

Instructions for Use:

1. Answer each question by circling the appropriate number.
2. Respond as close to your true feelings as possible.
3. If you do not have children, omit questions 1 and 48 and answer the alternate questions instead.
4. For negatively worded questions, circle "4" if you desire a positive response. (Example: If you regularly pray with your partner, answer Question 4 by circling "4.")

Answer Key:

1	2	3	4
(Almost) Always	Frequently	Sometimes	Rarely (Never)

Circle only one response for each item.

1. Children take your energy to the degree that you have little left for one another.   1   2   3   4
   Alternate Question: The question of whether to have children is a source of conflict in your marriage.   1   2   3   4

2. Do one or both of you travel frequently away from the home because of career?   1 2 3 4

3. You have trouble enjoying your sexual relationship.   1 2 3 4

4. You do not pray for or with each other.   1 2 3 4

5. Is jealousy an issue in your marriage?   1 2 3 4

6. Do you regularly complain, whine, or think negatively?   1 2 3 4

7. Do you feel frustrated or unsatisfied after discussing or attempting to discuss an important issue with your mate?   1 2 3 4

8. Do you disagree over seemingly insignificant events or issues?   1 2 3 4

9. Do you or your spouse feel excluded by one or both sets of parents?   1 2 3 4

10. Do you have trouble making ends meet financially?   1 2 3 4

11. In your marriage, one or both of you tend to look out for "Number One" before the partner.   1 2 3 4

12. There is sickness in the immediate or extended family.   1 2 3 4

13. Are you moody?   1 2 3 4

14. As you look back on your parents' marriage, would you say they were unhappy?   1 2 3 4

15. When you go out together, it is with others, not by yourselves.   1 2 3 4

16. When you embrace your spouse, do you feel emotionally distant?   1 2 3 4

17. Do you find it easier to discuss your feelings with another member of the opposite sex than with your spouse?   1   2   3   4

18. It is difficult for you to play-fully tease each other.   1   2   3   4

19. Do you question your spouse's love for you?   1   2   3   4

20. Do you question whether your mate really wants the best for you?   1   2   3   4

21. Do you experience extended periods of silence after an argument?   1   2   3   4

22. Do you doubt whether you really loved your spouse when you married?   1   2   3   4

23. Is your marriage characterized by dominance/submission?   1   2   3   4

24. You do not have clearly de-fined goals for your marriage.   1   2   3   4

25. Do you disagree on parenting philosophy and procedures?   1   2   3   4

26. Either one or both of you could be accused of being workaholics.   1   2   3   4

27. You disagree over the frequency and style of inter-course.   1   2   3   4

28. In your marriage you have trouble practicing forgiveness.   1   2   3   4

29. Do either or both of you have a tendency to be self-attack-ing or critical?   1   2   3   4

30. Do you have difficulty toler-ating or dealing with your spouse's differences?   1   2   3   4

31. Do you talk to friends about your feelings and marriage more than with your mate?   1   2   3   4

32. Does the marriage experience occasions of blaming, shouting, or accusing without finalizing anything?   1   2   3   4

33. Are there unresolved hard feelings with one or both sets of parents?   1   2   3   4

34. Are you in debt?   1   2   3   4

35. One or both of you can be accused of being selfish and self-centered.   1   2   3   4

36. Substance abuse (alcohol, drugs, overmedication) is an issue.   1   2   3   4

37. Is your spouse moody?   1   2   3   4

38. In your childhood, family members rarely expressed affection.   1   2   3   4

39. Your schedules are such that you rarely see each other.   1   2   3   4

40. There is very little romantic feeling.   1   2   3   4

41. Your spouse seems irritable and has had frequent unexplained absences.   1   2   3   4

42. Laughing together is unheard of.   1   2   3   4

43. Do you question your love for your spouse?   1   2   3   4

44. Do you experience periods of silence and/or ultimatums, threats, and sarcasm?   1   2   3   4

45. When you review the circumstances that played a part in your marriage, you think of more negative reasons than positive ones.   1   2   3   4

46. Does one partner make the decisions most of the time?   1   2   3   4

47. In practice, your joint married
    goals usually receive less
    attention than your individual
    desires.   1   2   3   4

48. Do you lose your temper with
    your children?   1   2   3   4
    Alternate question: Not having
    children is largely due to the
    instability of your marriage.   1   2   3   4

49. One or both of you is not
    satisfied sexually.   1   2   3   4

50. Your actions, in daily life,
    are frequently inconsistent
    with your spiritual beliefs.   1   2   3   4

51. Do either of you depend or
    lean on the other too much?   1   2   3   4

52. Do you find yourself trying to
    figure out, on your own, what
    your partner thinks or feels
    about things?   1   2   3   4

53. When you are together, the
    atmosphere is tense.   1   2   3   4

54. Are there social, financial, or
    vocational ties (or value differ-
    ences) with one or both sets of
    parents which cause friction?   1   2   3   4

55. Do you disagree over your
    financial practices and the
    use of your financial resources?   1   2   3   4

56. Do you have trouble trusting
    other people?   1   2   3   4

57. It seems like there is one
    negative problem after another
    that faces you.   1   2   3   4

58. Have you or your spouse ever
    visited with a friend or pro-
    fessional concerning emotional
    difficulties?   1   2   3   4

59. It takes effort for you to stir
    up warm feelings for either
    one or both of your parents.   1   2   3   4

60. You do not get away (day, weekend) as a couple as much as you need to.   1   2   3   4

61. You feel there is a lack of motivation by one or both of you to give or to sacrifice for the other partner.   1   2   3   4

62. Do you ever fantasize about a relationship with another person?   1   2   3   4

63. Would you be afraid to pull a practical joke on your partner?   1   2   3   4

64. You imagine yourself single and free from marriage and family obligations.   1   2   3   4

65. Is either one of you stubborn and/or self-willed?   1   2   3   4

66. Your job (outside or inside the home) causes significant stress for you.   1   2   3   4

67. Sex is a battleground.   1   2   3   4

68. You have trouble agreeing on your spiritual convictions and practices.   1   2   3   4

69. Do you react negatively (defend, attack, withdraw) when your partner offends you?   1   2   3   4

70. Do you feel taken advantage of by your partner?   1   2   3   4

71. Do you or your spouse not talk about feelings, beliefs, or issues in order to avoid potential conflict?   1   2   3   4

72. Do you have difficulty resolving disagreements?   1   2   3   4

73. You cannot agree on the level of involvement you want to have with your families (parents, siblings).   1   2   3   4

74. You have trouble trusting each other financially.   1   2   3   4

75. It is a problem for you to have your own friends outside of the marriage.   1   2   3   4

76. Do you suspect that you or your spouse have unresolved emotional or psychological difficulties?   1   2   3   4

77. Do you find it difficult to honestly say "I love you"?   1   2   3   4

78. Are you or your spouse more involved with outside interests (job, children, friends, hobby) than with your marriage?   1   2   3   4

79. You wish it was more fun to be at home.   1   2   3   4

80. You stay together more because of external reasons (beliefs, for the kids, money, family) than because you truly love and enjoy each other.   1   2   3   4

81. Do you and your spouse compete for control?   1   2   3   4

82. Do you mentally rehearse, "If only he/she would, then I would..."?   1   2   3   4

83. You are on edge about how your partner is going to respond to what you say and/ or do.   1   2   3   4

84. Is it difficult to consider your mate your best friend?   1   2   3   4

85. Do you keep from saying things because of previous misunderstandings, arguments, or frustrations?   1   2   3   4

Instructions for scoring and evaluation:

1. Total the numbers circled in answering the questionnaire.

2. Compare your score with the survey results by using the table below.

3. Read the description of each category following the table.

MAQ TABLE *

RANGE	CATEGORY
305-340	Optimal
275-304	Above Average
230-274	Average
200-229	Below Average
85-199	Dysfunctional

* Based on population sample results.

DESCRIPTION OF CATEGORIES:

Optimal: Couple functions exceptionally well together as individuals. They support, listen, and encourage each other and quickly resolve infrequent conflict. They deeply care for each other as they give and receive love.

Above Average: Happy with the relationship and care for each other. Negotiate well most of the time and display loyalty.

Average: Normal ups and downs. Relationship stressed occasionally and/or frequently. Struggles from outside plus misunderstandings and hurts from inside accompany pleasant, enjoyable experiences.

Below Average: Frequent difficulty. More downs than ups. Resentment, deep hurt, and extensive problems usually hound couple. Occasional times of pleasant exchange, but usually emotionally separated.

Dysfunctional: Unresolved, continuing difficulties. Abuse, despair, defeat, defensiveness and/or unhappiness. Relationship lacks skills and/or motivation to function.

Helpful Source Materials

Chapter 2

1. *National Study of Family Strengths*, by Nick Stinnet. University of Nebraska, 1981.
2. "Characteristics, Strengths of the 'Healthy' Family," by John Rosemond. *Des Moines Register*, July 22, 1984.
3. *Normal Family Processes*, by Froma Walsh. New York: The Guilford Press, 1982.
4. *Traits of a Healthy Family*, by Dolores Curran. Minneapolis: Winston Press, 1983.

Chapters 3-10

1. *Handbook of Marriage Counseling*, by Ben N. Ard, Jr., and Constance Ard. Palo Alto, CA: Science and Behavior Books, 1976.
2. *Klemer's Counseling in Marital and Sexual Problems*, by Robert F. Stahmann, Ph.D., and William J. Hiebert. Baltimore: The Williams and Wilkins Company, 1977.

Chapters 11 and 17

1. *Communication: Key to Your Marriage*, by H. Norman Wright. Glendale: Regal Books, 1974.
2. *More Communication Keys to Your Marriage*, by H. Norman Wright. Ventura: Regal Books, 1983.
3. *Alive and Aware*, by Sherod Miller, Elam W. Nunnally,

and Daniel B. Wackman. Minneapolis: Interpersonal Communication Programs, Inc., 1975.

4. *Mirages of Marriage*, by William J. Lederer and Don D. Jackson, M.D. New York: W. W. Norton & Company, 1968.

Chapter 12

1. *Telling Yourself the Truth*, by William Backus and Marie Chapian. Minneapolis: Bethany House, 1985.

Chapter 13

1. *The God-Players*, by Earl Jabay. Grand Rapids: Zondervan Publishing House, 1969.
2. *When I Say No, I Feel Guilty*, by Manuel J. Smith, Ph.D. New York: Bantam Books, 1975.

Chapter 14

1. *Healing for Damaged Emotions*, by David A. Seamands. Wheaton: Victor Books, 1984.
2. *Your Inner Child of the Past*, by W. Hugh Missildine, M.D. New York: Pocket Books, 1963.
3. *Psychotherapy and Growth*, by W. Robert Beavers, M.D. New York: Brunner/Mazel Publishers, 1977.

Chapter 18

1. *Your Money Matters*, by Malcom MacGregor. Minneapolis: Bethany House Publishers, 1977.
2. *Your Money Matters Workbook*, by Malcom MacGregor. Minneapolis: Bethany House Publishers, 1978.